Pray & Stay Connected to GOD

PATIENCE EMAMONI IWOH

 FriesenPress

Suite 300 - 990 Fort St
Victoria, BC, V8V 3K2
Canada

www.friesenpress.com

Copyright © 2019 by Patience Emamoni Iwoh
First Edition — 2019

Foreword by Pastor Dave Arogbonlo and Pastor Edidiong Udofia

ISBN
978-1-5255-3854-4 (Hardcover)
978-1-5255-3855-1 (Paperback)
978-1-5255-3856-8 (eBook)

1. Religion, Christian Life, Prayer

Distributed to the trade by The Ingram Book Company

TABLE OF CONTENTS

PROLOGUE

This book is a devotional prayer guide. It is based on fresh inspiration I have received from God in the course of my daily walk with Him. I have discovered that when I pray less, I get disconnected from God. I have also observed that many Christians today sometimes experience an unstable connection with God. They are in and out of fellowship with God. They can be on fire for God today and become lukewarm the next day.

This book is meant to help Christians pray and maintain a stable connection with God. There is so much evil happening in Christendom today that can make a Christian too easily disconnect from God. In the news, you hear about pastors judging and condemning other pastors, you hear about Christian marriages breaking up, and these happenings are against the will of God.

If a Christian is not properly rooted in the word of God and connected to God, he or she can easily lose faith. Imagine you are working on a school project on the internet and you have a strong Wi-Fi connection—it will be easier for you to access different websites for journals or books or articles, and you will have more information to help you finish the project on time. But if the Wi-Fi connection is poor, it will take longer to finish.

Imagine if a plant is firmly rooted to the ground through the taproot; it will receive the necessary nutrients from the soil to help it grow. But if the plant is not firmly rooted, it will lose nutrients and die.

For a believer to run the Christian race successfully and make it to heaven, we must have a stable connection to God, similar to a Wi-Fi connection, similar to the taproot of a plant, and remain connected to God so that He can lead and feed us. I pray that you will stay connected to God so that you can run the race well and make it to heaven in Jesus' name.

A Christian must stay connected to God because God is our source of power, our source of strength, and the closer we are to God the more strength we draw from Him. We can accomplish greatness through God. The Bible says:

"I am the vine, and you are the branches. If you stay joined to me, and I stay joined to you, then you will produce lots of fruit. But you cannot do anything without me."

John 15:5 Contemporary English Version (CEV).

"Apart from Christ a believer cannot accomplish anything of permanent spiritual value." Life Application Study Bible

I started writing this book on February 9, 2018; the thirtieth day of fasting and prayer in RCCG as I was led by God to write to encourage Christians to pray, depend on God, and stay connected to Him.

In the course of my walking with God, I have reflected on my life, upon my past failures and upon my successes, and I have discovered that everything I have achieved in life today is all by the grace to God. I have seen that the more I connect to God through prayer, the more I hear God speak to me, and the more I see God making a way for me. I have seen God make a way for me in so many situations in life.

God can also make a way for you, and you can achieve your goals by staying connected to Him. God is faithful always, and He is not a respecter of persons. I believe that God will make a way for you as you put your trust in Him by praying and connecting to Him.

I am putting this book together to encourage Christians to maintain regular fellowship with God to pray and stay connected. The book also provides insights into the reasons why a Christian should stay connected to God, the benefits of staying connected to God, and the dangers of disconnecting from God. There are also some prayer points based on the Bible to guide you to pray.

May the Lord bless you as you pray and stay connected to God in Jesus' name. Amen.

ENDORSEMENT

My precious wife, Patience, and I have been married for twenty-four years. I have known her to be a very passionate, praying woman who loves and fears God. Patience is passionate about prayers and leading group prayers at the family alter at home and with the extended family, at house fellowships, and in in the church.

Patience is also very passionate about spending quality time with God praying and studying God's word. Her passion for quality time made it possible for her to receive and to compose many prayer songs that she has ministered during prayer meetings in church and also many songs that she has taught the chosen generation children choir. Her zeal to serve God and mentor people propelled her to pioneer the chosen generation children choir, a forty-children choir group in RCCG House of Praise in Calgary. This is a group she started in 2010.

In this book she has shared her daily inspirations and prayer points in order to encourage people to cultivate a prayerful life and to strengthen their connections with God. This book is intended to help people pray and strengthen their connection to God. This book is meant to help you grow by studying to know God better and understand some common causes of disconnection so you can be aware and remain connected to God.

May the Lord bless you as you pray and stay connected to God.

Deacon James Iwoh, P.Eng.
RCCG House of Praise Calgary, Alberta

FOREWORD

It is with great joy that I commend this book to you on the subject so dear to the heart of God: prayer and staying connected with the Almighty. Deaconess Patience Iwoh doesn't merely talk about prayers, she prays. Serious prayers have to be birthed from God's eternal Word, energized by the Holy Spirit. If only we can all just stay connected better; if only we can enforce His mandate on us by depending just a little more on Him through prayer; if only we would just manifest our Sonship as He expects us to; if only we would be Word-ruled rather than sense-ruled…and I can go on.

May you pray and not sleep, for it's when men sleep that the adversary plants tares in lives (Mat 13:25). Those who know their God shall be strong and carry out great exploits (Dan 11:32). Prayer and staying connected to God makes you who He made you to be.

I am so glad that someone of this outstanding caliber is responding to the Divine call to wake up the people of God. As you read this book, may you recover all the grounds you have inadvertently surrendered to the enemy; may your voice be heard on high; may the Lord Himself boast of you as a Son, because that's who He has made all believers. May the slave spirit be flushed out of you (John 15:15); and may you be all that God has made you to be; and may you reign in life for Him (Rom 8:17). There's no better place for you to reign than in the place of prayer. And please remember this: A man that has learnt to be bowed before the Almighty in prayer will never be humiliated before mere men.

Go and prevail through prayer and staying connected with the Almighty.

Pastor Dave Arogbonlo
Senior Pastor
RCCG Living Word Chapel, Houston, Texas

Pray and Stay Connected to God is an inspiring book with a strong message that will benefit everyone who is open to it. The message in this book not only stresses the importance of prayers but the necessity of maintaining a stable, uninterrupted connection to God. Most believers are very good at praying, with most people approaching God only when they need something specific from Him. The importance of communication, which is the transmission of information between two people with understanding, cannot be overemphasized in any successful relationship. The same applies to our relationship with God. To further elaborate on this, beyond us talking to God through prayers, we need to give God an opportunity to speak to us as well by listening to him. There is no greater need in the church today than to mobilize Christians to move from practicing religion to having a stable connection with God.

A strong connection with God is essential if we are to experience everything He has in store for us. The Bible in 2 Corinthians 3:4-5 (GNT) says "[4] We say this because we have confidence in God through Christ. [5] There is nothing in us that allows us to claim that we are capable of doing this work. The capacity we have comes from God." God is the author of our lives and wants us to honor Him with it. To fully grasp what God has for us, it is pertinent that we are dedicated and committed to our relationship with God, ensuring that our connection with Him is clogged free as it is only through this that our motives are shaped.

Even though technology has made communication so easy, we are in a time where people, despite the number of friends and network on social media, are loneliest. This implies that beyond just communicating with God, it is essential to establish, strengthen, and maintain a viable connection with Him. In this book, Deaconess Patience Iwoh, with her deep insight into the word of God and passion for prayers, addresses a key challenge facing the body of Christ today and gives a solid course of action needed to activate, stabilize, and maintain our connections to God.

Jesus, our perfect example, made it crystal clear in John 15:5 that our choice is between connecting with God and being fruitful or not connecting with God and doing nothing of eternal significance with our lives. "Live in me. Make your home in me just as I do in you. In the same way that a branch can't bear grapes by itself but only by being joined to the vine, you can't bear fruit unless you are joined with me." John 15:4, MSG. The benefits of knowing God through His word, applying God's word, allowing God to speak to us through His word and responding to Him in prayer based on His word are unimaginable. Apart from providing a catalyst for unleashing the explosive power of our connection with God, Deaconess Patience Iwoh further elaborates on the SOAP format, which is very essential for every believer who seeks to stay connected with God.

As a pastor, I have discovered that most people truly and genuinely desire a reliable connection with God but simply don't have the tools to get and keep them there. The book you have in your hand, written by inspiration, is designed to take you through a proven process, guided by the Holy Spirit, of staying connected to God. Our dear sister Patience in doing this expounds the subject of prayer and connection to God with simplicity and incisiveness that would encourage any reader not just to go through the book but to yearn for a stable connection with God.

For every believer who desires to actualize the purpose of God for his or her life, this book is indispensable, and I commend it to our reading and practice. In reading this book, you will gain insights of the importance of a stable connection with God, which every believer should have, the dangers of disconnecting from God, as well as the lasting benefits of staying connected to God.

Pastor Edidiong Udofia
Senior Pastor, RCCG House of Praise Calgary, Alberta

DEDICATION

This book is dedicated to my wonderful husband of twenty-four years, Engineer James Iwoh, a minister of God. He has been my pillar and a strong support in my career and ministry. Also to our three wonderful children, Alexander, Jeffery, and Stephanie, and to my two lovely nieces, Anita Ikeh and Onyinyechi Ofonyeandi. To my sister Irene Sowho and the family, and to my brother Eboh Ewewe and the family.

To my in-laws, Mrs. Alice Okorodudu and the family, Solomon Iwoh and the family, Paul Iwoh and the family, Mabel Adeosun and the family. My family means everything to me. I love you all.

To all my children in the Chosen Generation Children Choir, House of Praise Calgary. May the blessing of the Lord continually be upon your lives in Jesus' name. May the Lord bless you and keep you all. May the Lord make His face to shine upon you, May the Lord be the glory and the lifter of your head. When men are been cast down, there shall be a lifting for you in Jesus' mighty name. Amen.

ACKNOWLEDGEMENTS

I give all glory to God, my father, my maker, my creator, who has given me the inspiration to start writing this book and has helped me daily to make my dream come true. Thank you, Lord.

I appreciate my spiritual father in the Lord, Pastor E. A. Adeboye AKA Daddy G.O and his wife, Pastor Mrs. Foluke. A. Adeboye AKA Mummy G.O, the general overseer of the redeemed Christian Church of God. Your life and ministry are my main source of inspiration. I get inspired each time I listen to my Daddy G.O preach his sermons. His life-transforming messages have transformed me to become who I am today.

I would also like to acknowledge my daddy, Pastor Dave Arogbonlo, and his wife, Pastor Mrs. Eunice Arogbonlo, the senior pastor of RCCG Living Word in Houston. Your leadership and mentorship helped me to discover my ministry. I learned humility, commitment to faithful service, and determination to excel from you.

I would like to acknowledge my pastor, Pastor Edidiong Udofia, and his wife, Pastor Mfon Udofia, pastor of RCCG House of Praise Calgary for providing the platform for me to serve in different ministries in the church and to grow in the service of the Lord. Thank you for your prayers, for your support and for help with the workers directorate ministry.

I also acknowledge Pastor Mike and his wife, Pastor Bola Oladosu, the assistant pastor of RCCG House of Praise Calgary and all the pastors, ministers, and workers of House of Praise Calgary. God bless you all for your labor of love.

Special Thanks

I want to say a big thank you to the members and staff of FriesenPress who have worked tirelessly to help me make this publication possible.

Special thanks to Christoph Koniczek, my publishing consultant with FriesenPress and to Nicole Leblanc, my publishing coordinator. Thanks to Samuel Froese, my publishing specialist and to the editorial team who worked faithfully to make sure this book is properly written and that the message is clearly passed across to the audience.

Thank you to all members of FriesenPress for making my dream of publishing this book a reality. May the Almighty God bless you richly.

CHAPTER 1
Introduction

Imagine you are connected to someone who is in authority of a nation, like Justin Trudeau, the prime minister of Canada, and imagine you are connected to Donald Trump, the president of the United States, or that you are connected to the Queen of England. What do you think you would stand to gain just because you know these people and you are connected to them?

Now imagine you are relating to the prime minister of Canada or the queen of England on a daily basis; how would this affect your life and your status? How would your relationship affect your access to privileged information?

Your relationship with the prime minister of Canada can give you some advantage in terms of having up-to-date information about policies and future plans for the government. There are many benefits you may get for yourself and for your family because you are connected to people in authority.

If your connection with a man can give you so much benefit, then think about the benefits your connection with God can bring to you and your entire generation. Now think about the efforts you will make to maintain such a relationship with the president or prime minister; think about how you got to know him—was it an introduction by a friend? How did you maintain your connection or your friendship with him? Was it by visiting him regularly or by communicating through telephone, Skype, WhatsApp, or Twitter? Maybe Facebook or other social media platforms? How did you maintain your connection with your prime minister or president?

In our world today, the prevalence of social media has made communication with people very easy; we can connect with our friends and family through various social media on mobile phones. Just as we make an effort to maintain our relationships with fellow men that were voted into office by us, we should also make an effort to maintain our relationship with the Almighty God, our creator. Our God is the King of Kings.

We can connect to God wherever we are by praying and by reading our Bible, just like we use social media. It is important that we spend time with God by studying His word and by praying so we can know God better.

I pray that as you read this book you will do your best to strengthen and maintain your relationship with God by praying and having regular fellowship with Him.

WHAT DOES IT MEAN TO STAY CONNECTED TO GOD?

To be connected means to be linked to someone or be joined together in a relationship.

According to Merriam-Webster's dictionary, connected means "joined or linked together, having the parts or elements logically linked together, related by blood or marriage, having social, professional, or commercial relationships."

In other words, to be connected means to have an intimate relationship with someone, either by socializing with them or by relating and communicating with them from time to time.

Staying connected to God means having an intimate relationship with God. It means having a regular communion of fellowship with God. This is very important for a Christian. Many of us today put in effort to connect to our friends daily through social media and we are eager to know what they are doing and how they are doing. This is perfectly okay in maintaining our relationships. We are happy, and our friends are also happy. At the same time, we need to put in effort to connect to God daily and be LinkedIn to God daily.

"I love this passage by an unknown author:

Stay connected. God has no phone, but I talk to Him

He doesn't have Facebook, but He is still my friend

He doesn't have Snapchat, but He knows my story

He doesn't have Instagram, but I still follow him.

As a believer, you ought to follow God even by listening to His voice and in that way we can stay connected to God."

In John 10:27, the Bible says:

"My sheep hear My voice, and I know them, and they follow Me."

New King James Version (NKJV).

In John 15:5, Jesus said:

"I am the vine, and you are the branches. If you stay joined to me, and I stay joined to you, then you will produce lots of fruit. But you cannot do anything without me."

Contemporary English Version (CEV).

To stay connected to God means to stay joined to God so you can live a good Christian life, a life that other believers can emulate and copy.

To stay connected to God means to remain in Christ. Remaining in Christ means:

(1) Believing that He is God's Son. 1 John 4:15

(2) Receiving him as Savior and Lord. John 1:12

(3) Doing what God says. 1 John 3:24

(4) Continuing to believe the Good News. 1 John 2:24

(5) Relating in love to the community of believers, Christ's body. John 15:12

Life Application Study Bible

"Many people try to be good, honest people who do what is right. But Jesus says that the only way to live a truly good life is to stay close to him, like a branch attached to the vine. Apart from Christ, our efforts are unfruitful. Are you receiving the nourishment and life offered by Christ, the vine? If not, you are missing a special gift he has for you."

Life Application Study Bible

WHY IS IT IMPORTANT FOR A CHRISTIAN TO STAY CONNECTED TO GOD?

It is our connection with God that empowers us to do God's will.

"For it is God who works in you both to will and to do for His good pleasure." Philippians' 2:13.

Staying connected to God means being filled with the Spirit of God. Samson was connected to God, and the Spirit of the Lord was moving upon him and he was able to do God's will. In Judges 13:24-25, the Bible states:

"So the woman bore a son and called his name Samson; and the child grew, and the LORD blessed him. ² And the Spirit of the LORD began to move upon him at Mahaneh Dan between Zorah and Eshtaol."

Our connection with God helps us to bear fruit. In John 15:5, the Bible says:

"I am the vine, you are the branches. He who abides in Me, and I in him, bears much fruit; for without Me you can do nothing."

Our connection with God helps us to experience the presence of God; in Psalm 91:1-2, the Bible says:

"He who dwells in the secret place of the Most High Shall abide under the shadow of the Almighty."

I will say of the Lord, "He is my refuge and my fortress; my God, in Him I will trust."

When you spend time with God, when you think about God, or when you write about God's word, you will experience the presence of God and strengthen your connection to Him. Our connection with God helps us to understand how God works. Moses was connected and He saw God at work in the burning bush.

Now, Moses was tending the flock of Jethro, his father-in-law, the priest of Midian. And he led the flock to the back of the desert and came to Horeb, the mountain of God. And the Angel of the Lord appeared to him in a flame of fire from the midst of a bush. So he looked, and behold, the bush was burning with fire, but the bush was not consumed. Then Moses said, "I will now turn aside and see this great sight, why the bush does not burn."

So when the Lord saw that he turned aside to look, God called to him from the midst of the bush and said, "Moses, Moses!"

And he said, "Here I am."

Then He said, "Do not draw near this place. Take your sandals off your feet, for the place where you stand is holy ground." Exo 3:1-5

WHAT CAUSES DISCONNECTION BETWEEN GOD AND MAN? CAUSES OF DISCONNECTION FROM GOD

A believer can disconnect from God without knowing it, so it is important to watch out for some of the reasons that can cause disconnection so we can carefully deal with the appearance of any of these factors.

The number-one cause of disconnection from God is sin.

Sin can cause a disconnection between man and God. When Adam and Eve sinned against God by eating the forbidden fruit, they were instantly disconnected from God, they became afraid of God, their loving Father and their creator, and they started covering their sin and hiding from God. In Genesis 3:8-13 the Bible states;

8 And they heard the [a]sound of the Lord God walking in the garden in the [b]cool of the day, and Adam and his wife hid themselves from the presence of the Lord God among the trees of the garden.

'9 Then the Lord God called to Adam and said to him, "Where are you?'

10 So he said, 'I heard Your voice in the garden, and I was afraid because I was naked; and I hid myself.'

11 And He said, 'Who told you that you were naked? Have you eaten from the tree of which I commanded you that you should not eat?'

12 Then the man said, 'The woman whom You gave to be with me, she gave me of the tree, and I ate.'

13 And the Lord God said to the woman, 'What is this you have done?'

The woman said, 'The serpent deceived me, and I ate.'"
NKJV

Because Adam and Eve sinned against God they began to hide and run away from the sweet fellowship they use to have with Him. When they were confronted by God, they refused to take responsibility for their actions and instead they apportioned blame to one another.

Have you ever found yourself in such a situation where you are hiding your sins from God? Or in a situation where you refuse to take responsibility for your sins? Have you ever found yourself blaming others for your sins?

The Bible gives so many examples of how sin has separated people from God. For example, King Saul was disconnected from God because of sin of disobedience, and God rejected him from being king. 1 Samuel 15:23, NKJV, in the Bible says:

"[23] For rebellion is as the sin of [a]witchcraft, and stubbornness is as iniquity and idolatry. Because you have rejected the word of the LORD, He also has rejected you from being king."

King David was also disconnected from God because of the sins of lust, adultery, and murder. Because of the love for pleasure, David was temporarily disconnected from God, but he later repented, and God had mercy on Him. David is called a man after God's heart:

1 Samuel 13:14: "He was God's choice of a king for his people."

In 2 Samuel 11:2-5, NKJV, the Bible states:

"[2] Then it happened one evening that David arose from his bed and walked on the roof of the king's house. And from the roof he saw a woman bathing, and the woman *was* very beautiful to behold. [3] So David sent and inquired about the woman. And *someone* said, '*Is* this not Bathsheba, the daughter of Eliam, the wife of Uriah the Hittite?' [4] Then David sent messengers, and took her; and she came to him, and he lay with her, for she was cleansed from her impurity; and she returned to her house. [5] And the woman conceived; so she sent and told David, and said, 'I *am* with child.'"

You have the right to refuse to sin, you have the power to resist sin, so you must guard against willful sin so you can continue to enjoy sweet fellowship with God. Sin can separate us from God; sin can lead to unanswered prayers. In Isaiah 59:1-3, NVJV, the Bible states:

"Behold, the LORD's hand is not shortened, that it cannot save; nor His ear heavy, that it cannot hear. But your iniquities have separated you from your God; and your sins have hidden His face from you, So that He will not hear. For your hands are defiled with blood, And your fingers with iniquity; Your lips have spoken lies, Your tongue has muttered perversity"

I read this beautiful explanation from the Life Application Study Bible, and it offers a deeper understanding about the impact of sin on our relationship with God.

Isaiah 59:1-14: "Sin offends our holy God and separates us from him. Because God is holy, he cannot ignore, excuse, or tolerate sin as though it didn't matter. Sin cuts people off from him, forming a wall to isolate God from the people he loves. No wonder this long list of wretched sins makes God angry and forces him to turn away. People, who die with their life of sin unforgiven, separate themselves eternally from God. God wants them to live with him forever, but he cannot take them into his holy presence unless their sin is removed. Have you confessed your sin to God, allowing him to remove it? The Lord can save you if you turn to him."

Another major cause of disconnection from God is prayerlessness. A prayerless Christian is a powerless Christian. You can become powerless because of lack of prayer because if you don't pray, you unplug yourself from your source of power. God is our source of power.

The Bible says in Psalm 62:11: "all power belongs to God.

God has spoken once, Twice I have heard this: That power belongs to God."

For a Christian to be powerful, you must connect to God through prayers. You must plug into that source of power. A powerless Christian is like an unplugged and uncharged computer; when a computer is not charged and it is unplugged, it will not work until you plug it into the source of power. And when you do, it will take time to charge and reboot before it can start working again.

If you turn away from your prayerlessness and return back to God, God will hear you. The Bible states in 2 chronicles 7:14, NKJV:

"If My people who are called by My name will humble themselves, and pray and seek My face, and turn from their wicked ways, then I will hear from heaven, and will forgive their sin and heal their land."

Another major cause of disconnection from God is wrong association. This can lead to sin, which ultimately separates us from God. In 2 Corinthians 6:14, NKJV, the Bible says:

"14 Do not be unequally yoked together with unbelievers. For what fellowship has righteousness with lawlessness? And what communion has light with darkness?"

It is important to choose your friends wisely and not to team up with unbelievers; it is dangerous to team up with unbelievers because if you are not careful, you will lose your faith.

On the other hand, if you are led and empowered by God to win that unbeliever to Christ, you can associate with them. In 1

Corinthians 9:19-22, we are encouraged by apostle Paul to serve all men.

"19 For though I am free from all men, I have made myself a servant to all, that I might win the more; 20 and to the Jews I became as a Jew, that I might win Jews; to those who are under the law, as under the law, that I might win those who are under the law; 21 to those who are without law, as without law (not being without law toward God, but under law toward Christ), that I might win those who are without law; 22 to the weak I became as weak, that I might win the weak. I have become all things to all men, that I might by all means save some."

CHAPTER 2

How to Stay Connected to God

HOW DO I STAY CONNECTED TO GOD?

- Examine yourself
- Check your connection to God
- Plug in if you were unplugged

EXAMINE YOURSELF

"Test and evaluate yourselves to see whether you are in the faith and living your lives as [committed] believers. Examine yourselves [not me]! Or do you not recognize this about yourselves [by an ongoing experience] that Jesus Christ is in you—unless indeed you fail the test and are rejected as counterfeit? ⁶ But I hope you will acknowledge that we do not fail the test nor are we to be rejected. ⁷ But I pray to God that you may do nothing wrong. Not so that we [and our teaching] may appear to be approved, but that you may continue doing what is right, even though we [by comparison] may seem to have failed."

2 Corinthians 13:5-7 Amplified Bible (AMP)

Assess your connection to God

Take this short quiz to assess your level of connectedness to God

1. Do you love God? Yes / No
2. Do you love sin? Yes/ No
3. Do you get involved in sinful habits sometimes (lying, backbiting, jealousy, envy)? Yes /No
4. Do you love to pray? Yes / No
5. Do you pray regularly, at least up to 3 times a day? Yes / No
6. Do you enjoy praying corporate prayers? Yes / No
7. Do you pray corporate prayers with a group daily? Yes / No
8. Do you enjoy listening and singing praises to God regularly? Yes / No
9. Do you enjoy reading the Bible daily? Yes/ No
10. Do you listen to audio or video sermons regularly? Yes / No
11. Do you enjoy fellowshipping with other believers?

Check your responses to determine how connected you are to God.

If you answered "YES" up to six or eight times, it shows you are making good effort to connect and stay connected to God daily. If you answered "NO" to the questions up to seven or eight times, it indicates your connection to God is unstable. If your connection is unstable, then try and fix it by rebooting your system, or try to plug in again if you were unplugged.

"Test yourselves to make sure you are solid in the faith. Don't drift along taking everything for granted. Give yourselves regular checkups. You need firsthand evidence, not mere hearsay, that Jesus Christ is in you. Test it out. If you fail the test, do something about it. I hope the test won't show that we have failed. But if it comes to that, we'd rather the test showed our failure than yours.

We're rooting for the truth to win out in you. We couldn't possibly do otherwise.

We don't just put up with our limitations; we celebrate them, and then go on to celebrate every strength, every triumph of the truth in you. We pray hard that it will all come together in your lives."

2 Corinthians 13:5-9, The Message (MSG)

HOW DO I STAY CONNECTED TO GOD?

- Regular prayer
- Regular fasting
- Regular study of God's word
- Regular fellowship with God's people

HOW DO I STAY CONNECTED TO GOD?

1. Stay connected to God in prayer. Fasting, personal prayers, the family altar, and corporate prayers can increase your connectivity with God.

    "However, this kind does not go out except by prayer and fasting."
    Matthew 17:21, NKJV

    Fasting and prayer is an important way to stay connected to God. Fasting is a time when you seek God's face in prayer, deny yourself of your usual pleasure, and focus on God alone.

2. Stay connected to God by studying the word of God. Let God speak to your heart. When possible, use your Bible to study and highlight key scriptures.

3. Stay connected to God in Fellowship. These days, with the effectiveness of social media, everything is now online so people don't even bother to go to church anymore. But there is a difference between watching service online and being present physically.

Values are changing rapidly. For instance, there is the transgender and gay movement and so on. We need to stay connected with God so we can maintain our faith and live a life that is pleasing to God.

When you are connected to God then He will become your exceeding great Reward. If you are connected to God, you are sure of divine protection. When you are connected to a God, you carry His presence and you are sure that God will be your exceeding great reward.

"After these things the word of the LORD came to Abram in a vision, saying, "Do not be afraid, Abram. I am your shield, your exceedingly great reward.

Genesis 15:1, NKJV

Prayers

- *Father, help me to remain connected to you*
- *Help me to live above the distractions and attractions of the world*
- *Show me the ways of life.*

Start today by practicing constant conversation with God and continual mediation on his Word. Prayer lets you speak to God; mediation lets God speak to you. **Rick Warren**

STAY CONNECTED TO GOD: REMAIN IN HIS PRESENCE IN PRAYERS.

- Stay joined to Christ
- Make effort to remain in His presence
- You will accomplish things of permanent spiritual value

"I am the vine, you are the branches. He who abides in Me, and I in him, bears much fruit; for without Me you can do nothing. If anyone does not abide in Me, he is cast out as a branch and is withered; and they gather them and throw them into the fire, and they are burned. If you abide in Me, and My words abide in you, you will ask what you desire, and it shall be done for you."
John 15:5-7, NKJV

In the above scripture, we were told that God is the husbandman, Jesus is the vine, and we believers are the branches in Christ.

"Stay joined to me, and I will stay joined to you. Just as a branch cannot produce fruit unless it stays joined to the vine, you cannot produce fruit unless you stay joined to me. I am the vine, and you are the branches. If you stay joined to me, and I stay joined to you, then you will produce lots of fruit. But you cannot do anything without me. If you don't stay joined to me, you will be thrown away. You will be like dry branches that are gathered up and burned in a fire. Stay joined to me and let my teachings become part of you. Then you can pray for whatever you want, and your prayer will be answered."

John 15:4-7, CEV

"In verse 15:5-6, staying connected to God or Remaining in Christ means (1) believing that he is God's Son (1 John 4:15), (2) receiving him as Savior and Lord (John 1:12), (3) doing what God says (1 John 3:24), (4) continuing to believe the Good News (1 John 2:24), and (5) relating in love to the community of believers, Christ's body (John 15:12)."

Life Application Study Bible

Apart from Christ, a believer cannot accomplish anything of permanent spiritual value.

Not abiding in Christ has serious consequences:

(1) The person **is cast out as a branch,** indicating the loss of fellowship.

(2) The person **is withered,** indicating a loss of vitality.

(3) The person is **burned,** indicating a loss of reward. **The fire** here is figurative, symbolizing either fiery trials (see 1 Pet. 1:7; 4:12) or the fire at the judgment seat of Christ (see 1 Cor. 3:11–15). Failure to abide produces spiritual disaster. They gather them and thrown into the fire to burn.

Copied from NKJV Study Bible.

Your connection with God in regular fellowship matters, and it makes a lot of difference. For example, Abraham was connected to God, and that was why God spoke to him personally, and that is why God called him His friend.

In Gen 15:1, NKJV, the Bible says:

"After these things the word of the LORD came to Abram in a vision, saying, "Do not be afraid, Abram. I am your shield, your exceedingly great reward.""

Do you want God to speak to you personally? Are you connected to God? If you are disconnected, you won't hear when God speaks. It is important to stay connected to God so God can speak to you.

In Psalm 27:4, the psalmist says:

"One thing I have desired of the LORD, That will I seek: That I may dwell in the house of the LORD All the days of my life, To behold the beauty of the LORD, And to inquire in His temple."

When we spend time in God's presence and seek his face, we strengthen our relationship with God.

Place your desires before God. Pray about them and trust God to give them to you if and when they're right for you. **Joyce Meyer**

STAY CONNECTED TO GOD: PRAY WHEREVER YOU ARE

- Pray wherever you are
- Pray about anything
- Believe in your prayers
- God answers prayers

When you pray, something happens:

"Therefore I say to you, whatever things you ask when you pray, believe that you receive them, and you will have them."

Mark 11:24, NKJV

I believe in prayers and I enjoy praying. I know that when you pray and believe in your prayers, God hears and answer them. If you believe in what you are praying about, you will receive it.

God always answer prayers, and I have seen the result of answered prayers in my life so many times. In March 2018, While I was doing my teaching practicum, I had a burden to pray concerning my end of practicum report, because I was worried that I was teaching few classes in a day, I was worried because I felt that if I teach more classes, my supervisor will be happy with me and rate me well. So I prayed and prayed and decreed concerning the report. I engaged myself in regular prayers, praying at home and praying on my way to work and praying silently at work. And on the day that I received my report, I was surprised to see that exactly what I prayed for, was what my supervisor wrote in my end of practicum evaluation. I was really happy and I thanked God for the good report. To God be the glory.

When you pray something happens, you can pray even under any condition. Prayers require your determination and commitment.

Daniel prayed regularly even though the king made a decree that no one should pray. God gave Daniel the spirit of excellence because of His connection with God. Daniel was able to interpret dreams that wise men could not interpret the dream because God revealed this deep secret to Him. God gave Daniel wisdom and strength.

In Daniel Chapter 2:17-23 the Bible says;

"[17] Then Daniel went to his house, and made the decision known to Hananiah, Mishael, and Azariah, his companions, [18] that they might seek mercies from the God of heaven concerning this secret, so that Daniel and his companions might not perish with the rest of the wise men of Babylon. [19] Then the secret was revealed to Daniel in a night vision. So Daniel blessed the God of heaven.

[20] Daniel answered and said:

'Blessed be the name of God forever and ever,

For wisdom and might are His.
[21] And He changes the times and the seasons;
He removes kings and raises up kings;
He gives wisdom to the wise
and knowledge to those who have understanding.
[22] He reveals deep and secret things;
He knows what is in the darkness,
and light dwells with Him.
[23] 'I thank You and praise You,
O God of my fathers;
You have given me wisdom and might,
And have now made known to me what we asked of You,
For You have made known to us the king's [a] demand.'
NKJV

When you pray, God can reveal things to you through vision, just as He revealed the secret of the king's dream to Daniel through night vision.

The presence of God was mighty upon Daniel because he was prayerful and connected to God.

If you believe in prayer at all, expect God to hear you. If you do not expect, you will not have. God will not hear you unless you believe He will hear you; but if you believe He will, He will be as good as your faith. **Charles Spurgeon**

PRAY IN A QUIET PLACE

- Spend time alone with God
- Listen to God speak
- Let God instruct and teach you

BIBLE PASSAGE

"Now in the morning, having risen a long while before daylight, He went out and departed to a solitary place; and there He prayed." Mark 1:35, NKJV

In the above scripture we are told that Jesus went to a quiet place to pray. It is sometime very difficult to get time alone with God. But we are advised to follow the example of Jesus in Mark 1:35.

"Jesus' prayer life was successful because it was planned, private, and prolonged. He got up early enough, got far enough away, and stayed at it long enough."

Life Application Study Bible

"It's easy to be so caught up with ministry that you neglect times of solitude, individual worship, and prayer. Perhaps you need to redesign your schedule to find time for earnest prayer. It is vitally important to:

(1) Seek the Lord before your busy schedule takes over your thoughts; (2) withdraw from noise and demands so you can focus on God;

(3) Take Jesus' attitude of regular communion with the Father;

(4) Reflect on the priorities Jesus had for his life;

(5) Determine to pray on a more regular basis, not just in times of crisis. If prayer was important for Jesus, then it must be important for his followers. Pray—even if you have to get up very early in the morning to do it!"

Life Application Study Bible

Quiet time alone with God is very important in the life of a believer. Most Christians do not hear or receive a word from God because they are too busy. I was also a victim of this, but now I have learned to pray in a quiet place. I enjoy praying in the early morning as soon as I wake up, and I enjoy having a personal retreat; a time to be alone with God.

I remember a time came in my life when I decided to be alone with God and have a personal retreat while on vacation in Orlando Florida in 2016. I was tired of sickness and doctor's reports I was getting when my son was sick. The reports were not pleasant to hear, so I decided to let go of everything I wanted to do that night. I let go of my sleep, I let the kids go to bed without unnecessarily begging them to eat before bed, and I let my husband sleep so I was alone and could commune with God.

And God began to speak to my heart, and I began to write as God spoke to me concerning that situation. He reassured me that He would take care of me and my family.

Spending time with God is the key to our strength and success in all areas of life. Be sure that you never try to work God into your schedule, but always work your schedule around Him. Joyce Meyer

In Psalm 32:8, NKJV, the Bible says:

"I will instruct you and teach you in the way you should go;

I will guide you with My eye."

Another version of the Bible states that:

"The Lord says, 'I will guide you along the best pathway for your life.

I will advise you and watch over you.'"

Psalm 32:8, NLT

In Psalm 32:8, God exhorts us not to be stubborn like horses or mules that have to be controlled by bits and bridles. If we comply with God's guidance, he will not have to resort to applying discipline and punishment to keep us on track. God longs to guide us with love and wisdom rather than punishment. He offers to teach us the *best* way to go. Accept the advice written in God's Word and don't let your stubbornness keep you from obeying God.

Regular prayers in a quiet place help us to hear the voice of God.

God wants to "do life" with you. That means He wants to be involved in every area, on your heart and mind, all day long. As you give Him your attention, He will speak to your heart and guide you with His wisdom. **Joyce Meyer**

GUARD YOUR HEART

- Think pure thoughts
- Delete impure thoughts

"Keep your heart with all diligence, For out of it spring the issues of life."

Pro. 4:23, NKJV

The heart is very delicate; it needs to be conditioned regularly so it doesn't crack or break. Guard your heart with God's word, guard your heart with prayers and meditation on the word of God. Guard your heart by asking the Holy Spirit for grace to sanctify, preserve, and keep your heart.

Beloved, we need to guard our hearts because God searches the heart.

In Jeremiah 17:10, NKJV, the Bible says:

"I, the LORD, search the heart, I test the mind, Even to give every man according to his ways, According to the fruit of his doings."

The heart is so deceitful and wicked, we need to guard it to ensure that it is focused on the right path of life. In our day-to-day life, we see different things, hear different things and think about different things; the human brain is constantly working every minute. I have discovered that I am always thinking of something, either good or bad.

In the past I have entertained thoughts of failure, of limitations, of hereditary diseases, and these fears affected my life. In the early 90s I saw a manifestation of some of these fears. In early 2000 while I was in Oman, I was always sick. I had a terrible lower-left-hand-side pain that came on and off, and for which I always found myself in the hospital. I thought it was a hereditary disease, so I was living in fear. But as I grew in the knowledge of God's word, His word purified my heart, and today I can live without that unnecessary fear—and I am pain free. The way we think and what we think about matters, and it makes a lot of difference in our life.

If you keep thinking about failure and inability to do anything, it is very likely to experience failure. If you keep thinking about your limitations, it is very likely to experience limitation and live a limited life. On the contrary, if you think about success and breakthroughs and meditate on those thoughts of success, you will be likely to experience success and breakthroughs in life.

The life of Job in the Bible is a classical example of someone who was thinking of failures, trials, and fears of the unknown. He experienced trials and his fears became real.

Job 3:25 says that when Job was afflicted, he exclaimed that his fear has become real.

"For the thing which I greatly feared is come upon me, and that which I was afraid of is come unto me." Job 3:25-26. KJV

It is very important to guard your heart and control the thoughts that go through your mind. You are the master of your mind, and you have the right to accept good thoughts and reject or delete bad or negative thoughts. The earlier you delete bad thoughts from your mind, the better for you. After deleting them, you can start conditioning your heart to start thinking pure thoughts.

The way you think determines the way you feel, and the way you feel determines the way you act. **Rick Warren**

The Bible says:

"Finally, brethren, whatsoever things are true, whatsoever things are honest, whatsoever things are just, whatsoever things are pure, whatsoever things are lovely, whatsoever things are of good report; if there be any virtue, and if there be any praise, think on these things."
Philippians 4:8, KJV

Prayer:

Lord, please help me to keep my heart. Help to think pure thoughts in Jesus' name. Amen.

God will not accept a divided heart. He must be an absolute monarch. There is not room in your heart for two thrones. You cannot mix the worship of the true God with the worship of any other god more than you can mix oil and water. It cannot be done. There is not room for any other throne in the heart if Christ is there. If worldliness should come in, godliness would go out. **Dwight L. Moody**

DEPEND ON GOD

- Obey God's leading
- Do not question God
- Take God by His word

BIBLE PASSAGE

"I am the vine, you are the branches. He who abides in Me, and I in him, bears much fruit; for without Me you can do nothing."
John 15:5

On the 13th of January 2017, while I was preparing for a workers' prayer meeting, the Lord gave me this word: Depend on Me." Prophesies had been released for the year, and 2017 was declared a year of surprises by the general overseer of RCCG, Pastor E.A Adeboye. And in our local parish, House of Praise Calgary, it had been declared a year of greater heights. God said to me that to receive pleasant surprise from Him and also get to greater heights, I must depend on Him.

What does it mean to depend on God? How do I depend on God? When you hear the word "depend," what comes to your mind? To depend means to be controlled or determined by. Be contingent on, be conditional on, be dependent on, hinge on, hang on, rest on, rely on; be decided by.

The opposite of depend is mistrust and to question.

So God is saying hang on me, rely on me, let me decide for you, be dependent on me. You don't need to question God because God is unquestionable; you don't need to mistrust God because

God is trustworthy. You don't need to limit God because God is unlimited.

What does it mean to depend on God? Does it mean that you don't have to make any plans for yourself? No. To depend on God means to trust God with all that you have. Abraham depended on God, he trusted God with everything He had. When God asked Abraham to go and sacrifice his only son, Abraham obeyed God without questioning Him.

In Genesis 22:1-4, NKJV, God said to Abraham:

"Now it came to pass after these things that God tested Abraham, and said to him, 'Abraham!'

And he said, 'Here I am.'

Then He said, 'Take now your son, your only son Isaac, whom you love, and go to the land of Moriah, and offer him there as a burnt offering on one of the mountains of which I shall tell you.'

So Abraham rose early in the morning and saddled his donkey, and took two of his young men with him, and Isaac his son; and he split the wood for the burnt offering, and arose and went to the place of which God had told him. Then on the third day Abraham lifted his eyes and saw the place afar off."

To depend on God means God is in charge and controls your day-to-day affairs while you live in total obedience to Him.

Prayer:

Lord, help me to depend on You by living a life of total obedience to You.

Depend on God power, not willpower **Rick Warren**

RELY ON GOD

- God is faithful to His promise
- He is a reliable God
- He is the same God yesterday, today and forever

Bible verse
"⁹ God is faithful [He is reliable, trustworthy and ever true to His promise—He can be depended on], and through Him you were called into fellowship with His Son, Jesus Christ our Lord."
1 Corinthians 1:9, Amplified Bible

In this era of economic crisis, religious crisis, and political crisis, when men are faced with so many challenges of life, there is a tendency to question if God is aware of all that is going on. Christians may be tempted to want to believe the question posed by the psalmist in Psalm 42:3 that states: "My tears have been my meat day and night, while they continually say unto me, where is thy God?"

Psalm 115:2: "Why should the gentiles say where is their God?"

The answer to this question is found in Psalm 115:3: "but our God is in heaven; He does whatever He pleases."

It may seem like your dreams are not been realized as expected. You may be facing a challenge today and wonder when you will overcome this challenge. I want you to know that God has a word for you. Our God is reliable; He will fulfill His promises towards you when you rely on Him. We need to rely on God now always. A lot of Christians today are facing one challenge or the other; some are faced with unemployment, some are faced with single parenting, late marriage, bareness and infertility. I want you to know that you can rely on God because He has a word for you.

When faced with challenges of life, whom do you run to? Do you run to the phone or run to the throne? You may run to men, but a man can fail you. The Bible says it is better to put your trust in God because God never fails. In Psalm 118:8, the Bible says: "8 It is better to trust in the LORD than to put confidence in man."

It is only God that can give you the answer to life's most difficult questions. So why worry when all you need to do is to trust God? You may not have everything that the world has to offer—that dream career, that dream home, the perfect family. You may not have the riches that the world has to offer but you can rely on God. The Lord gave me a word on January 12, 2017, the second day of RCCG forty days of fasting and prayer, and that word became my song for that day and for the week. The word is that Jesus is more than enough for me.

Below are the lyrics to the song that God gave to me:
You are more than enough for me
You are more than enough, Lord Jesus
Everything that I need
I find in you
You are more than enough for me.
God's grace is more than enough for us;
through Jesus you can do all things.
Trust in the Lord because His word is yes and Amen.

"20 For all the promises of God in Him *are* yes, and in Him Amen, to the glory of God through us."
2 Corinthians 1:20, NKJV

The Lord gave me this song in October 2016:
You are reliable, God
You are reliable, God
The same God yesterday is the same today

Reliable Reliable God
Reliable Reliable God

In my walk with God I have experienced that God is truly reliable. The Bible says in numbers 23:19 that God cannot lie—He is reliable. "God is not a man, that He should lie, Nor a son of man, that He should repent. Has He said, and will He not do? Or has He spoken, and will He not make it good?"

Beloved God is reliable; you can depend on God, and He is the very present help in time of trouble.

In Psalm 46, verse 1-5, King James Version, the Bible says:

"God is our refuge and strength, a very present help in trouble.

[2] Therefore will not we fear, though the earth be removed, and though the mountains be carried into the midst of the sea;

[3] Though the waters thereof roar and be troubled, though the mountains shake with the swelling thereof. Selah.

[4] There is a river, the streams whereof shall make glad the city of God, the holy place of the tabernacles of the most High.

[5] God is in the midst of her; she shall not be moved: God shall help her, and that right early."

God is truly reliable and dependable.

Prayer

I pray that you will connect and depend on God because He is reliable. I pray that you will arise from your challenges and from every difficulty of life and shine today in Jesus' name.

Prayer lets you speak to God; meditation lets God speak to you. Both are essential to becoming a friend of God. **Rick Warren, *The Purpose Driven Life: What on Earth Am I Here For?***

STUDY GOD'S WORD AND APPLY IT

SOAP format:

- Search the scripture
- Observe the scripture
- Apply the scripture
- Pray the scripture

Use SOAP regularly to wash yourself so you can stay connected to God. **Patience Iwoh.**

STUDY GOD'S WORD AND APPLY IT

"Study to show thyself approved unto God, a workman that needeth not to be ashamed, rightly dividing the word of truth."
2 Timothy 2:15, King James Version

Read the Bible, study it to know God's word. Read different versions, read it with understanding, read it for application.

Study the word of God to know God's promises so you can lay claim to these promises.

Study to understand the truth of the word of God

The scriptures are given not to increase our knowledge, but to change our lives. **Dwight L. Moody**

"[8] This Book of the Law shall not depart from your mouth, but you[a] shall meditate in it day and night, that you may observe to do according to all that is written in it. For then you will make your way prosperous, and then you will have good success."
Joshua 1:8, NKJV

You can study the Bible using different Bible=study formats.

You can use the SOAP format. SOAP stands for Scripture, Observation, Application and prayer:

S-Scripture: Here is where you write down a verse frome your reading that stood out for you. Copy it word for word with citation.

O-Observation: Here you answer the question, "what do I observe about this verse? Who is speaking? To whom? Where? Why?"

A-Application: How can I apply this verse to my life or how does it apply to a present situation?

P-Prayer: What prayer does this inspire me to praise God with? What prayer could I pray asking God for?

In our prayers, we talk to God, in our Bible study, God talks to us, and we had better let God do most of the talking. **Dwight L. Moody**

Everyone ought to study the Bible with two ends in view: his own growth in knowledge and grace, and passing it on to others. We ought to have four ears, - two for ourselves, and two for other people. My Bible is worth a good deal to me because I have so many passages marked that, if I am called upon to speak at any time, I am ready. We ought to be prepared to pass around heavenly thoughts and truths, just as we do the coin of the realm. **Dwight L. Moody**

MAKE YOURSELF AVAILABLE TO GOD

"[8] Then I heard the voice of the Lord saying, 'Whom shall I send? And who will go for us?'

And I said, 'Here am I. Send me!'"

Isaiah 6:8, New International Version

The Lord spoke to me about the importance of making oneself available to Him. During one of my church's monthly pastors and ministers meeting, God spoke to me and challenged me to make myself available to Him. God gave me this song during the meeting, and I have used this song to encourage God's people during my ministration. Meditate on the lyrics of this song. The message here is simply to make yourself available to God so He can use you for His glory.

Song
Lord, I'm available to you
Lord, I'm available to you
Use me for your glory,
I am available to you.
Use me for your glory,
I am available to you.
Lord, I'm available to You
Lord, I'm available to you
Lord, I'm available to you
Use me for your glory,
I am available to you.
Use me for your glory,
I am available to you.

CHAPTER 3
Dangers of Disconnecting from God

THE SPIRIT OF THE LORD WILL DEPART FROM YOU

"But the Spirit of the LORD departed from Saul, and a distressing spirit from the LORD troubled him."
    1 Samuel 16:14, NKJV

"Saul was rejected as King over Israel because He disobeyed God's instruction to go and destroy the Amalekites."
    1 Samuel 15:3.
"Saul disobeyed the instruction by sparing the King and some animals"
    1 Samuel 15:9.
"Because of this disobedience, Saul was rejected as king. In 1 Samuel 16:4, we are told that the Spirit of the Lord left king Saul. The Spirit of the Lord means the spirit of prophecy, the spirit of wisdom and prudence in civil government, and the spirit of fortitude and courage. And in place of the Spirit of the Lord, an evil Spirit from the Lord troubled Him as a punishment for his sins. He became distracted in his counsels, and became weak and foolish, lost all courage and greatness of mind, was timorous and

fearful and alarmed by everything and was full of envy, suspicion, rage and despair." (Copied from John Gill's exposition on the whole Bible).

It is a dangerous thing to disconnect yourself from God. When you disconnect from God and remain disconnected, it will become impossible for you to fulfill your destiny. According to Tony Evans, "If you disconnect your life from God, you disconnect yourself from your destiny."

So many Christians have ended their lives without fulfilling their destinies. Just like King Saul, they started well but ended their Christian race poorly.

Reflection

Please take a moment to reflect on your walk with God and ask yourself, am disconnecting from God? Or am I still connected to God? Is the Spirit of God still at work in my life? Am I exhibiting the wisdom and courage that is an evidence of the Spirit of God in me?

Prayer

Father Lord please do not reject me, please do not take away the Holy Spirit from me, help me to stay connected to you and never to disconnect from You in Jesus name I pray.

THE POWER OF GOD WILL DEPART FROM YOU

²⁰ And she said, "The Philistines *are* upon you, Samson!" So he awoke from his sleep, and said, "I will go out as before, at other times, and shake myself free!" But he did not know that the LORD had departed from him." Judges 16:20, NKJV

Samson was given a divine assignment before He was born. Judges 14:1-16 gives an account of how the angel of the Lord appeared to Samson's mother and told her that she who has been barren will become pregnant and have a son and the son will be a nazarite from the mothers womb.in Judge 14:2-6 the Bible says;

"Now there was a certain man from Zorah, of the family of the Danites, whose name *was* Manoah; and his wife *was* barren and had no children. And the Angel of the LORD appeared to the woman and said to her, "Indeed now, you are barren and have borne no children, but you shall conceive and bear a son. Now therefore, please be careful not to drink wine or *similar* drink, and not to eat anything unclean. For behold, you shall conceive and bear a son. And no razor shall come upon his head, for the child shall be a Nazirite to God from the womb; and he shall begin to deliver Israel out of the hand of the Philistines."

Judges 13:2-5, NKJV

The purpose or calling of God upon the life of Samson was to deliver Israel from the Philistines, but he could not deliver Israel because he was disconnected from God. The love of women derailed his vision and purpose and He became disconnected from God. Samson got entangled with a strange woman called Delilah who deceived Him with love and made him to reveal the secret of His God given strength. As soon the woman heard of this secret she cut off his hair and Samson lost his power. In Judges 16:20 we were told that Samson did not know that the power of God has departed from Him. And he was delivered to his enemies who tormented him greatly and plucked out his eyes. Samson, who was so powerful, was reduced to a prison and a grinder of corn in the prison. Samson died without fulfilling his God-given purpose.

Reflection

Do you have a divine assignment or purpose? Are you connected to God so you can fulfill that assignment? Has the Lord anointed you? Or are ordained by God for an assignment? Are you taking the anointing or ordination of God for granted? Are you serious with the calling that God has called you are you taking that assignment that God gave to you for granted?

Beloved brethren, it is time to wake up and strengthen your connection with God. Do not disconnect from God.

Prayer

My Father and my God, please help me to remain connected to You. Deliver me from any entanglement with sin. Help me, Lord, to take the assignment You have given to me seriously. Help me to fulfill the purpose for which you have created me. Help me not to be distracted form serving you, oh God. In Jesus mighty name I pray. Amen.

YOU BECOME A SLAVE TO SIN

It happened in the spring of the year, at the time when kings go out *to battle,* that David sent Joab and his servants with him, and all Israel; and they destroyed the people of Ammon and besieged Rabbah. But David remained at Jerusalem.

"2 Then it happened one evening that David arose from his bed and walked on the roof of the king's house. And from the roof he saw a woman bathing, and the woman *was* very beautiful to behold. 3 So David sent and inquired about the woman. And *someone* said, 'Is this not [a]Bathsheba, the daughter of [b]Eliam, the wife of Uriah the Hittite?' 4 Then David sent messengers, and took her; and she came to him, and he lay with her, for she was cleansed from her impurity; and she returned to her house. 5 And the woman conceived; so she sent and told David, and said, "I *am* with child.'"

2 Samuel 11:1-5, NKJV

David was supposed to be in the battleground fighting for victory for God's people, but he decided to stay back home. He started to seek pleasure when he suddenly saw a woman bathing. He inquired about her and was told who she was. David was so disconnected from God at this moment that he didn't know what he was doing. He sent for her and slept with her, not minding that she was the wife of Uriah the Hittite. They both committed adultery and the result was pregnancy. David became a slave to sin because he was at the wrong place at the wrong time.

In order to cover up for the sin of adultery, David connived with the leader of the army to commit murder; he instructed Joab, the commander of the army, to place Bathsheba's husband Uriah in the hottest part of the battle so he could be killed. What a wicked act. This instruction was carried out and Uriah died, and then King David married Bathsheba, who was already pregnant with child.

At this point of David's life he was so disconnected from God; so disconnected that even when the Man of God, Nathan, came with a message from God to rebuke King David, David did not see himself in the picture of the message that was delivered to him, but rather he pronounced judgment on the man who had committed this great sin. He didn't realize the message was directed to him until the prophet Nathan told him, "You are the one."

In 2 Samuel 12:5-10, the Bible says:

5 So David's anger was greatly aroused against the man, and he said to Nathan, "*As* the LORD lives, the man who has done this [a] shall surely die! 6 And he shall restore fourfold for the lamb, because he did this thing and because he had no pity."

7 Then Nathan said to David, "You *are* the man! Thus says the LORD God of Israel: 'I anointed you king over Israel, and I delivered you from the hand of Saul. 8 I gave you your master's house and your master's wives into your keeping, and gave you the house of Israel and Judah. And if *that had been* too little, I also would have given you much more! 9 Why have you despised the commandment of the LORD, to do evil in His sight? You have killed Uriah the Hittite with the sword; you have taken his wife *to be* your wife, and have killed him with the sword of the people of Ammon. 10 Now therefore, the sword shall never depart from your house, because you have despised Me, and have taken the wife of Uriah the Hittite to be your wife.'"

When you disconnect from God, and fall into sin, you will think you are enjoying life, but the truth of the matter is that you are living in bondage to sin.

Reflection

Do you sometimes find yourself in a situation when you refuse to be where God wants you to be at a particular time? What are some of the consequences of this kind of disobedience? Have you ever found yourself being rebuked and you don't even know it?

That is how dangerous it can be when you disconnect from God. You become a slave to sin and its consequences.

Have you ever found yourself in a web of sin where the result of one sin leads to a greater sin? How often do you try to cover your sin? Remember that God sees everything we do.

Prayer

Father, please give me the grace to be in the right place at the right time, in Jesus' name.

Lord, please help me to exercise complete dominion over sin.

I declare that sin shall not have dominion over me in the name of Jesus'.

Father, help me not to cover my sins, oh God, help me to confess my sins whenever I fall into sin.

Give me the grace to live above sin.

May I never become a slave to sin, in Jesus' name.

CHAPTER 4
Benefits of Staying Connected to God

ABILITY TO DO ALL THINGS THROUGH CHRIST

Bible verse:

"I can do all things through Christ, which strengthens me."
Philippians 4:13, KJV

I read the Bible commentary from the Life Application Study Bible and the commentary really made me to think about the scripture above. Can we really do everything? We may not be able to do everything on our own, but the power we received from our union with Christ is enough for us to do His will and to face the challenges we may face in life. We will be faced with trials and temptations, but when we look up to God and ask for strength, we will be able overcome any difficulty.

In the passage above, Apostle Paul said he could do all things through Christ; that he has learned in the course of time to depend on God for everything and in every situation, whether in the good times or in the bad times.

In the course of my walk with God, I have learned to depend on Him, and I can confidently say that I can do all things through

Christ who strengthens me. I can write new songs through Christ who strengthens me, I can teach and sing new songs that I have composed through Christ who strengthens me. I can only do these things through Christ, because I have a relationship with Christ, and I am abiding in Christ and connected to Him.

Do you have a desire to do all things through Christ? Are you connected to Christ? If so, you can do all things through Him. If you desire to do all things through Him then you need to connect with Christ by receiving Him as Lord and savior into your life. After receiving Christ into your life then you can abide in Him and do all things through Him.

I can do all things through Christ who strengthens me because God is on my side. The Bible says if God be for us who can be against us?

"what then shall we say to these things? If God is for us, who can be against us? Romans 8:31, NKJV

God loves us with an everlasting love and He wants us to live life in abundant. We only need to connect with God.

Romans 8:31, NKJV

You may have a dream of doing great things for God, for your church, for your community; a dream of becoming a world changer, a dream of impacting your generations with God's blessings. If you are limited in one way or the other, I want you to be rest assured that you can do all things through Christ who strengthens you.

In my Christian walk I have seen and experienced God working in me and through me in diverse ways. The Lord unleashed the gift of songwriting in my life in the year 2003, and in the year 2016 the Lord was faithfully releasing new songs to me on a regular basis. God gave me the opportunity to minister the songs as well.

In 2106 the Lord gave me the song "Lord, I'm Available to You," which I ministered for the first time during one of our ministers' meeting. Just after I received the Lord, I shared it with the pastors and ministers. Afterwards I also ministered the song to the workers during our early morning prayer. I can only do these things through Christ.

In December 2016, while I was preparing the CCGC for Christmas carol night, the Lord reminded me of the new songs He had given to me. I went through my personal songbook to select two new songs that God inspired me to compose and I began to teach the children at CCGC. To my surprise, the children were so excited about the new songs, and they sang with enthusiasm. That gave me confidence that God was going to do something great with the CCGC on that carol night.

We continued to practice these songs in our choir rehearsal and the children ministered the songs on the carol night. People were blessed; it was so glorious. Glory be to God. While preparing for the children's manifest Sunday, for May 7, 2017, God gave me a song for the theme of the program: "Pressing to a Greater Height." The song is titled "We are Going to a Greater Height." I was blessed as the children's choir rendered this song. Here are the lyrics:

We are going higher and higher,
We are going to greater heights,
Nothing can stop us
because God is with us.
We are going to greater height.
Higher higher
Higher higher
Higher higher
We are going to greater height.

The children's choir and I practiced the song several times and ministered it on the manifest Sunday, May 7, 2017. To God be the glory for the great things He has done.

On my own I cannot do any of these things, but because God was on my side, I could write the song and teach the children and also coordinate the children to sing the song. I can do all things through Christ who strengthens me.

Prayer

Lord, please help me to depend on you to help me do all things through Christ, in Jesus' name I pray.

Action: Write Your Personal reflection

Think about a time in your life that God has given you the leading to write a book or a song or a message. Has God asked you to minister to a group of people? Think about how God helped you to do this.

GOD WILL GIVE HIS ANGELS CHARGE OVER YOU

Bible verse

"For He shall give His angels charge over you, To keep you in all your ways." Psalms 91:11 .

Do you ever feel unsecured? Do you ever feel lonely? I want you to know that God has given his angels an assignment concerning you, and that assignment is to keep you in all your ways. So whenever you feel lonely or insecure, remember Psalm 91:11.

We live in a dangerous world surrounded by evil. There is so much going on: suicide bombing, plane crashes, assassinations, and kidnapping, but God has made provisions for the safety of His people. The angels of God are there to keep you in all your righteous ways, so you need to walk righteously to enjoy this protection from them.

In Psalm 91, verse 1-6, NKJV, the Bible states that:
"He who dwells in the secret place of the Most High
Shall abide under the shadow of the Almighty.
I will say of the LORD, 'He is my refuge and my fortress;
My God, in Him I will trust.'
Surely He shall deliver you from the snare of the fowler
And from the perilous pestilence.
He shall cover you with His feathers,
And under His wings you shall take refuge;
His truth shall be your shield and buckler.
You shall not be afraid of the terror by night,
Nor of the arrow that flies by day,
Nor of the pestilence that walks in darkness,
Nor of the destruction that lays waste at noonday."

The reality of this verse always comes to mind when I go on a journey, especially if I'm travelling by air. I realized that it is the presence of the guiding angels of God that guarantees my safety always.

I can testify that God has given His angels charge over my family and me because He has faithfully kept us in our journey to Nigeria and back to Canada during the summer vacations of 2016 and 2017.

The Bible says God will give His angels charge over me. "For He shall give His angels charge over you, To keep you in all your ways." Psalms 91:11

I can testify that God is faithfulness to His Word. He has given His angels charge over me and my family in all our ways. God is indeed the promise keeper. I thank God for safety and journey mercies by road and by air for members of our family. God, You are my keeper. Thank You, Lord, for giving your angels charge over me and my family. Lord, I am grateful. In Jesus' name I pray. Amen.

Action points

I want you to take a moment and think about one instance when you felt the presence of the angels of God around you. Think about it and thank God for giving His angels charge over you. Write your personal reflection. Think about how God has protected you and your family.

Prayer points

I thank you, Lord, for daily protection and safety. Thank you, Lord, for journey mercies on flights as I travel from coast to coast. Thank you, Father. I pray for protection for all those who are travelling and for those planning to travel by road, by air, and by sea. Please grant them safety and journey mercies, in Jesus' name.

Oh Lord, please give your angels charge over them, in Jesus' name I pray. And may we always have a reason to testify of your goodness and mercies, in Jesus' name I pray. Amen.

YOUR BURDEN WILL BE LIFTED

"Cast your burden on the LORD, and He shall sustain you; He shall never permit the righteous to be moved."
Psalms 55:22, NKJV

Beloved, I want you to know that God is your burden bearer, so cast that burden on the Lord so that you can be free. He can lift your heavy burden. If you cast your burden on the Lord, He will carry it for you. What is that burden that you carry today that makes you cry? Is it the burden of sickness, the burden of sin, the burden of sorrow, the burden of loneliness, the burden of financial difficulty? Cast that burden on the Lord and He will lift it and sustain you.

What does it mean to cast your burden on the Lord? It means to trust God to carry your burden for you so you don't carry it alone. Brothers and sisters, why are you still carrying that burden alone, when God can carry it for you? Why are you still carrying the burden of financial difficulties alone? Why are you still carrying the burden of sin alone when God can carry it for you? Why are you still carrying the burden of grief alone when God can carry it for you? Why are you still carrying the burden of loneliness alone when God can carry it for you?

Why carry your burdens alone when God can carry them for you? When you can cast your burden on the Lord and be free?

Are you carrying your burdens alone? And do you feel like your friends have forsaken you? If you have been carrying your burdens alone, it is time to give your burden to the Lord. If you feel like your friends have forsaken you, it is time to turn to God. Because God is the only true friend we have. He is a friend who never fails. He will carry your burdens. He is our burden bearer. Cry to God today and ask Him to take away the burden.

The Bible makes me to understand that God can take away burdens of long-standing problems. In the book of John 5:1-8, the Bible gives an account of how God lifted the burden of sickness and loneliness from a man who was sick for thirty-eight years.

John 5:1-8 states: "After this there was a feast of the Jews, and Jesus went up to Jerusalem. Now there is in Jerusalem by the Sheep Gate a pool, which is called in Hebrew, Bethesda, having five porches. In these lay a great multitude of sick people, blind, lame, paralyzed, waiting for the moving of the water. For an angel went down at a certain time into the pool and stirred up the water; then whoever stepped in first, after the stirring of the water, was made well of whatever disease he had. Now a certain man was there who had an infirmity thirty-eight years. When Jesus saw him lying there, and knew that he already had been in that condition a long time, He said to him, 'Do you want to be made well?' The sick man answered Him, 'Sir, I have no man to put me into the pool when the water is stirred up; but while I am coming, another steps down before me.' Jesus said to him, 'Rise, take up your bed and walk.'"

John 5:1-8, NKJV

From this we can see that the sick man was in one spot because of his sickness. He could not move forward when Jesus came into the scene, and Jesus asked Him, "Do you want to be made whole?" And the response the man gave to Jesus was so amazing.

He said, "I have no man to put me in the pool." In other words, he was saying to Jesus, "I am so lonely here." It looked like his friends and family had forsaken him. Do you sometimes feel like your friends and family have forsaken you? Many of us may feel lonely and without help sometimes but remember that God is always with you. Then Jesus healed him of that sickness and of His loneliness. The sick man who had been in one spot was now able to move around and worship freely. In John 5:14, it was recorded that Jesus later saw this young man in the temple.

I pray for you today that the burden that has made you lonely and has kept you in one spot shall be taken away, in Jesus' name.

I pray that your financial burden shall be lifted; the Lord will send you destiny helpers to meet your financial needs, in Jesus' name

I pray that the burden of marital confusion and storm shall be lifted, in Jesus' name.

I pray that the burden of diseases and sickness and the burden of long-standing problems shall be lifted, in Jesus' name.

IT SHALL BE WELL WITH YOU

"Say to the righteous that it shall be well with them, for they shall eat the fruit of their doings."
Isaiah 3:10, NKJV

Brothers and sisters, God is saying to you today that in that career where you have laboured, you will enjoy the result of your labour. What does it mean to eat the fruit of your doing? It means to enjoy your labour. The Bible says:
"In all labor there is profit, but idle chatter leads only to poverty."
Proverbs 14:23 NKJV

At that job in which you have been working so hard, you will have profit, in Jesus' name.

You will enjoy the fruit of your labour over your children, in Jesus name. I pray for you today that God will bless the work of your hands.

"Blessed shall you be in the city, and blessed shall you be in the country. "Blessed shall be the fruit of your body, the produce of your ground and the increase of your herds, the increase of your cattle and the offspring of your flocks. "Blessed shall be your basket and your kneading bowl. "Blessed shall you be when you come in, and blessed shall you be when you go out. "The LORD will cause your enemies who rise against you to be defeated before your face; they shall come out against you one way and flee before you seven ways."

Deuteronomy 28:3-7, NKJV

Let's look at the life of Isaac.

"Then Isaac sowed in that land, and reaped in the same year a hundredfold; and the LORD blessed him."

Genesis 26:12, NKJV

May the Lord bless you as you sow precious seeds of faith, in Jesus' name. May you have a bountiful harvest, in Jesus' name. Just like Isaac, may the Lord cause you to reap a hundred-fold, in Jesus' name.

GOD WILL FAITHFULLY COMPLETE THE GOOD WORK HE HAS STARTED IN YOUR LIFE

"Being confident of this very thing, that He who has begun a good work in you will complete it until the day of Jesus Christ;"

Philippians 1:6, NKJV

I pray for you today that God who has started a good work in you will complete it, in Jesus' name.

That project you started this year shall be completed, in Jesus' name. You will not leave it uncompleted, in Jesus' name.

It doesn't matter the pressure you are facing right now; don't give up on your project, and don't give up on your dream. Don't give up on your desires. Please patiently allow God to complete what He has started in your life.

Sometimes in life we feel incomplete because we are yet to see our big dream come true, but please don't give up.

You may be believing God for a miracle child and because of this you may feel incomplete. My dear brothers and sisters, do not let your situation define who you are.

The Bible says we are complete in Christ, with nothing missing and nothing broken.

"And you are complete in Him, who is the head of all principality and power."
Colossians 2:10, NKJV

Do not feel inferior because you don't have children.
Do not feel inferior because you are not yet married.
Do not feel inferior because you do not have a job.
Do not feel inferior because you are sick.

God is faithful to completing the good work He has started in you.
It is the will of God that you have children, so God will do it for you.
It is the will of God that you get married, so God will do it for you.
It is the will of God that you get a job, (God's desire is that you prosper), so He will do it for you.

I pray for you today that any situation that makes you feel incomplete the Lord God Almighty will turn around in the name of Jesus.

I pray that the sickness that makes you to feel incomplete will be terminated in the name of Jesus.

I decree and declare according to the word of God in Genesis 1:28 "Then God blessed them, and God said to them, 'Be fruitful and multiply.'"

I pray that you will be fruitful and you will multiply, in Jesus' name.

I decree and declare that the work of your hands shall be blessed, in Jesus' name. Amen.

GOD WILL HELP YOU

"For the Lord GOD will help me; therefore I will not be disgraced; therefore I have set my face like a flint, and I know that I will not be ashamed."

Isaiah 50:7, NKJV

Brother and sisters, I want you to know that the Lord God Almighty is able to help you; He is able to help you in that situation you find yourself right now.

The same God who commanded the ravens to feed Elijah at the brook of Cherith in the time of famine and drought, the same God can meet you at your point of need, he can provide for you, He is able to meet your needs. He is able to send you help from an unusual source. That is why God calls Himself "The I AM that I AM." He is the All Sufficient God; He can provide for your needs. He can help you in any situation you find yourself.

The Bible states:

³ "Get away from here and turn eastward, and hide by the brook Cherith, which flows into the Jordan. ⁴ and it will be that you shall drink from the brook, and I have commanded the ravens to feed you there."

1 Kings 17:3-4, NKJV

Now, my understanding about ravens is that they are very stingy birds and they will never give their food to anyone. But God commanded the ravens to carry food to his servant Elijah— isn't that amazing? That is what only God can do.

He can command help to you from an unusual source; a source that you least expect. I pray that God will command help for you from an unusual source, in Jesus' name.

I pray for you that in this season, God will help you,
And you will not be ashamed in the name of Jesus.
God will take away shame from your life.
God will cover you with his glory.
The garment of shame shall be taken away.
God will give you a garment of praise.

God is able to help you in any situation in which you find yourself. That is why the psalmist says:

"I will lift up my eyes to the hills— From whence comes my help? My help comes from the LORD, Who made heaven and earth."

Psalms 121:1-2, NKJV

Brothers and sisters, I want you to put your hope in the Lord. I want you to trust God to help you with your needs.

I want you to make your boast in the Lord that God is your helper. The Bible says:

"Some trust in chariots, and some in horses; But we will remember the name of the

Lord our God. They have bowed down and fallen; but we have risen and stand upright."
Psalm 20:7-8, NKJV

When you make your boast in the Lord, the Lord will show up for you. The Lord will show up for you in the nick of time. It doesn't matter what you are going through; know for sure that God is going to help you. God will send you destiny helpers to help you in the journey of life, in the name of Jesus.

I pray for you today that the Lord God Almighty will help you and you will not be disgraced. Because you have set your face on the Lord, you will not be disgraced, in Jesus' name. Anything and everything that brings shame the Lord will take far away from you in the mighty name of Jesus.

I decree and declare over your life that the Lord God Almighty will clothe you with garments of praise in the mighty name of Jesus. The Lord will take away every garment of shame in the mighty name of Jesus.

The Lord God will help you in life's journey; don't be disappointed, don't be discouraged, the Lord will help you, He is your helper, He will send destiny helpers your way to help you. Hold onto God trust in Him, and He will see you through.

If you are going to a place you have not been to before, fear not, God will help you.

When you are down to nothing, God is up to something.

When you find yourself in a difficult situation, let this be your disposition: "God will help me."

When you cannot speak for yourself, God will help you.

When you cannot provide for yourself, God will help you.

ALL THINGS WILL WORK TOGETHER
FOR YOUR GOOD.

"And we know that all things work together for good to those who love God, to those who are the called according to His purpose."
Romans 8:28, NKJV

Do you love God? How much do you love God? If you love God, you will love your neighbour; if you love God so much, you will love your neighbour so much. You will love people around you, your friends, colleagues, and because you love God and love the people around you, God will cause everything happening in your life surrounding you to work together for your good.

Now, it doesn't matter if you are going through a bad situation or a good situation; it doesn't mean God has forgotten you. God is still at work even when things are bad. God is still at work. He is working behind the scene to make everything beautiful. Let's look at the story of Joseph in Genesis 37:

The Bible records that Joseph's brothers hated him. They hated him because he had a dream, a dream of greatness, and he had a goal, he had a future. He told his brothers about his vision for life, and they hated him more, and they sold him into slavery, but because God has not finished with him, God picked him up and established him as a prime minister in Egypt.

That can also be your testimony. You may be hated by your brothers and sisters, your family members, your friends or your colleagues. They might despise you, but I want to encourage you to know that God has not finished with you because God is working behind the scene to make everything beautiful. I pray that in his time, he will make all things beautiful for you, in Jesus' name. I pray for you that God will cause everything that is working against you to turn around for your good, in Jesus' name.

God will touch your life; He will cause things to begin to work for you, in Jesus' name.

I pray that things will begin to work in your favour, that God will add favour to your labour.

In Jesus' name.

Romans 8:28 "God works in everything—not just isolated incidents—for our good. This does not mean that all that happens to us is good. Evil is prevalent in our fallen world, but God is able to turn every circumstance around for our long-range good. Note that God is not working to make us happy, but to fulfill his purpose. Note also that this promise is not for everybody. It can be claimed only by those who love God and are called by him, that is, those the Holy Spirit convinces and enables to receive Christ. Such people have a new perspective, a new mind-set. They trust in God, not in life's treasures; their security is in heaven, not on Earth. Their faith in God does not waver in pain and persecution because they know God is with them."

GOD WILL MAKE A WAY FOR YOU

Bible verse

"Behold, I will do a new thing Now it shall spring forth; Shall you not know it? I will even make a road in the wilderness And rivers in the desert."

Isaiah 43:19, NKJV

God is in control of our lives no matter what we are going through today. He will make a way for you. He will help you.

God says He will make a road in the wilderness and rivers in the desert. Can you beat that? Our God is so wonderful. I want you to know that God is in control of everything going on in your life. No matter what you have gone through in the past, no matter what you are going through today, God is in control and He has given us His word in Isaiah 43:19 that He will make a way. Everyone has moments of discouragement, but the only way out of discouragement is to trust God to make a way for you. I like this popular quote by Billy Graham that states:

"The Christian life is not a constant high. I have my moments of deep discouragement. I have to go to God in prayer with tears in my eyes, and say, 'O God, forgive me,' or 'Help me.'"

No matter what has happened, I want you to trust God and trust His word. He is able to make a way for you; the word of God is true, the word of God is sure. I encourage you to trust God, lift up your eyes to the Lord. In Psalm 121:1-6 the psalmist says:

"1 I will lift up my eyes to the hills—

From whence comes my help?

² My help comes from the LORD,

Who made heaven and earth.

³ He will not allow your foot to be moved;

He who keeps you will not slumber.

⁴ Behold, He who keeps Israel

Shall neither slumber nor sleep.

⁵ The LORD is your keeper;

The LORD is your shade at your right hand.

⁶ The sun shall not strike you by day,

nor the moon by night."

I encourage you to lift up your eyes unto God because He alone is the source of your help. Why don't you hold onto the word of God today because it's going to come through for you. He will make a way for you where there seem to be no way. Trust God because His word is yes and Amen. In 2 Corinthians 1:20, the Bible says:

"[20] For all the promises of God in Him are yes, and in Him Amen, to the glory of God through us."

I pray God's promises concerning your life will come to pass, in Jesus' name.

On November 4, 2017, the Lord gave me this song

He will see you through it all

He will see you through it all

Where there is no way, God will make a way

He will see you through it all

He will see you through it all

Prayer

Everlasting Father, king of glory. Thank you for your promise to make a way for me. Please make a way for me in every area where I am experiencing challenges right now. Please make a way for me, take control of every situation and have your way in my life, in Jesus' name.

REFLECTION

Is God in control of everything you are going through?

GOD'S PROMISES FOR YOU WILL COME TO PASS.

"For I know the thoughts that I think toward you, says the LORD, thoughts of peace and not of evil, to give you a future and a hope." Jeremiah 29:11, NKJV

God has good plans for you. God has good plans for you and for your career, and God has good plans for your marriage. God has good plans for your children. I want you to trust God so the good plans he has for you can materialize and come to pass in your life. I pray that God's plans for you shall come to pass, in Jesus' name. I pray for you that the word of God concerning you in in Jeremiah 29:11 will come to pass in your life, in Jesus' name. Amen.

You need to trust God so His good plans can come to pass in your life. You need to trust in God.

In the Book of Proverbs 3:5-6, the Bible says:
"5 Trust in the LORD with all your heart, and lean not on your own understanding; 6 in all your ways acknowledge Him, and He shall direct your paths."
Proverbs 3:5-6, NKJV

When you put your plans in the hands of God, He directs you, He takes you step by step and leads you to the place of rich fulfillment and leads you to the place of your destiny.

I encourage you to put your plans in the hands of God. It is normal for us human beings to have our own plans and to even not ask God about our plans. We have our plan A, plan B, plan C to implement, and it is only after we fail and face disappointment that we run back to God and cry for help. But it is even better when you start planning; invite the Lord, trust in Him, and ask God to plan with you. Put your plans in the hands of the Lord, and God will take you step by step to the place of rich fulfillment. I pray that God will take you to a place of rich fulfillment as you invite Him to plan with you, in Jesus' name.

Our God hears us. He answers prayers when we call upon Him; He hears and answers us. I pray for you that the promise of God in Jeremiah 29:11 will come to pass in your life, in Jesus' name. The promise of God concerning you that says you shall be the head and not the tail in Deuteronomy 28: 13 will come to pass in your life, in Jesus' name.

"And the LORD will make you the head and not the tail; you shall be above only, and not be beneath, if you heed the commandments of the LORD your God, which I command you today, and are careful to observe them."

The promise of God concerning your children in Isaiah 8:18 shall come to pass for you and your children, in Jesus' name. The Bible says:

"Here am I and the children whom the LORD has given me! We are for signs and wonders in Israel From the LORD of hosts, who dwells in Mount Zion."

Isaiah 8:18, NKJV

I pray that all the promises of God concerning you shall surely come to pass. Every promise of God that you are holding on to will surely come to pass for you and your family, in Jesus' name. Amen.

PRAYER

As you go out today, God will go with you. God will be in the centre of your plans and I pray that God will direct your plans and establish you, in Jesus' name. Amen.

Action

Write your personal reflection. Think about how God has fulfilled His promises in your life.

GOD WILL MAKE A WAY FOR YOU

"Behold, I will do a new thing, Now it shall spring forth; Shall you not know it? I will even make a road in the wilderness And rivers in the desert."
   Isaiah 43:19,NKJV

God has made a way for me on different occasions. In the early years of my marriage, the enemy began to wage war with me concerning childbearing. During that period we fought battles upon battles, and God gave victory upon victory. When the doctor said it was impossible for me to conceive and have a child, God made a way for me. I became pregnant and had a son who is twenty-three years old today. To God be the glory.

He made a way in the wilderness of my life and created a river in my desert places.
   I can testify today that God is a way-maker and a miracle worker.

I read the story of Pastor Travis Green, a songwriter and a musician; a Grammy-award winner that wrote the song "You Made a Way." When Travis Greene entered into this world stillborn, he was declared dead. His mama – Minister Charleather Greene – called on the name of the Lord and He answered and brought her baby boy back to life. At the age of four Travis fell out of the window of the family's fourth-floor apartment in Germany.

Someone advised his mom that her toddler was dead, and by the time she got outside a white sheet was pulled over his face. As she picked up the lifeless body of her child, she called on Jesus over and over until he came back to life.

This transpired in the natural world, but in the supernatural is an occurrence that has forever made an indelible imprint in the life of Travis Greene. As he fell from the window a giant hand accompanied by a very bright light caught him. The voice asked, "Do you want to go with your mom or do you want to come home with me?"

Four-year-old Travis answered, "I want my mom."

The voice said, "OK, go home to your mom, but the next time, you're coming home with me."

Inquisitively, Travis asked, "Sir, what is your name?"

The voice answered, "My name is Jesus."

The same God who made a way for me, who delivered me from barrenness, is the same God who made a way for Travis Greene and delivered him from death. This same God can make a way for you. Because God is not a respecter of persons. The Bible states clearly in the book of Acts that God is not a respecter of persons:

"[34] Then Peter opened his mouth, and said, of a truth I perceive that God is no respecter of persons:

[35] But in every nation he that feareth him, and worketh righteousness, is accepted with him."

Acts 10:34-35, King James Version (KJV)

Action point

I want you to take a moment and just think about one instance when you thought there was no way, and then suddenly God made a way for you. Think about it and begin to thank God.

Prayer points

1. *My Father and my God, please make a way for me in the areas where there seems to be no way.*
2. *Father, please make a way for me in the wilderness of my life, and create a river in desert places for me.*

Praying the Names of God

NAMES OF GOD FROM THE OLD TESTAMENT:

YOU ARE ELOHIM: Genesis 1:1, Psalm 19:1
Meaning "God," a reference to God's power and might.

YOU ARE ADONAI: Malachi 1:6
Meaning "Lord," a reference to the Lordship of God.

YOU ARE JEHOVAH–YAHWEH: Genesis 2:4
A reference to God's divine salvation.

YOU ARE JEHOVAH-MACCADDESHEM: Exodus 31:13
Meaning "The Lord thy sanctifier"

YOU ARE JEHOVAH-ROHI: Psalm 23:1
Meaning "The Lord my shepherd"

YOU ARE JEHOVAH-SHAMMAH: Ezekiel 48:35

Meaning "The Lord who is present"

YOU ARE JEHOVAH-RAPHA: Exodus 15:26
Meaning "The Lord our healer"

YOU ARE JEHOVAH-TSIDKENU: Jeremiah 23:6
Meaning "The Lord our righteousness"

YOU ARE JEHOVAH-JIREH: Genesis 22:13-14
Meaning "The Lord will provide"

YOU ARE JEHOVAH-NISSI: Exodus 17:15
Meaning "The Lord our banner"

YOU ARE JEHOVAH-SHALOM: Judges 6:24
Meaning "The Lord is peace"

YOU ARE JEHOVAH-SABBAOTH: Isaiah 6:1-3
Meaning "The Lord of Hosts"

YOU ARE EL-ELYON: Genesis 14:17-20, Isaiah 14:13-14
Meaning "The most high God"

YOU ARE EL-ROI: Genesis 16:13
Meaning "The strong one who sees"

YOU ARE EL-SHADDAI: Genesis 17:1, Psalm 91:1
Meaning "The God of the mountains or God Almighty"

YOU ARE EL-OLAM: Isaiah 40:28-31
Meaning "The everlasting God"

NAMES OF GOD FROM THE OLD
AND NEW TESTAMENTS:

YOU ARE ABBA: Romans 8:15

YOU ARE THE ADVOCATE: I John 2:1

YOU ARE THE ALMIGHTY: Genesis 17:1

YOU ARE ALPHA: Revelation 22:13

YOU ARE AMEN: Revelation 3:14

YOU ARE ANCIENT OF DAYS: Daniel 7:9

YOU ARE THE ANOINTED ONE: Psalm 2:2

YOU ARE THE APOSTLE: Hebrews 3:1

YOU ARE THE ARM OF THE LORD: Isaiah 53:1

YOU ARE THE AUTHOR OF LIFE: Acts 3:15

YOU ARE THE AUTHOR OF OUR FAITH: Hebrews 12:2

YOU ARE THE BEGINNING: Revelation 21:6

YOU ARE THE BLESSED & HOLY RULER: 1 Timothy 6:15

YOU ARE THE BRANCH: Jeremiah 33:15

YOU ARE THE BREAD OF GOD: John 6:33

YOU ARE THE BREAD OF LIFE: John 6:35

YOU ARE THE BRIDEGROOM: Isaiah 62:56

YOU ARE THE BRIGHT MORNING STAR: Revelation 22:16

YOU ARE THE CHIEF SHEPHERD: 1 Peter 5:4

YOU ARE THE CHOSEN ONE: Isaiah 42:1

YOU ARE CHRIST: Matthew 22:42

YOU ARE CHRIST OF GOD: Luke 9:20

YOU ARE CHRIST THE LORD: Luke 2:11

YOU ARE CHRIST, SON OF LIVING GOD: Matthew 16:16

YOU ARE THE COMFORTER: John 14:26

YOU ARE THE COMMANDER: Isaiah 55:4

YOU ARE THE CONSOLATION OF ISRAEL: Luke 2:25

YOU ARE THE CONSUMING FIRE: Deut. 4:24, Heb. 12:29

YOU ARE THE CORNERSTONE: Isaiah 28:16

YOU ARE THE COUNSELOR: Isaiah 9:6

YOU ARE THE CREATOR:1 Peter 4:19

YOU ARE THE DELIVERER: Romans 11:26

YOU ARE THE DESIRED OF ALL NATIONS: Haggai 2:7

YOU ARE THE DOOR: John 10:7

YOU ARE THE END: Revelation 21:6

YOU ARE ETERNAL GOD: Deut. 33:27

YOU ARE THE EVERLASTING FATHER: Isaiah 9:6

YOU ARE THE FAITHFUL & TRUE: Revelation 19:11

YOU ARE THE FAITHFUL WITNESS: Revelation 1:5

YOU ARE FATHER: Matthew 6:9

YOU ARE THE FIRSTBORN (3): Rom.8: 29,Rev.1: 5,Col.1: 15

YOU ARE THE FIRSTFRUITS: 1 Cor.15: 20-23

YOU ARE THE FOUNDATION: 1 Cor. 3:11

YOU ARE THE FRIEND OF TAX COLLECTORS SINNERS: Matthew 11:19

YOU ARE THE GENTLE WHISPER: 1 Kings 19:12

YOU ARE THE GIFT OF GOD: John 4:10

YOU ARE THE GLORY OF THE LORD: Isaiah 40:5

YOU ARE GOD: Genesis 1:1

YOU ARE GOD ALMIGHTY: Genesis 17:1

YOU ARE GOD OVER ALL: Romans 9:5

YOU ARE GOD WHO SEES ME: Genesis 16:13

YOU ARE THE GOOD SHEPHERD: John 10:11

YOU ARE THE GREAT HIGH PRIEST: Hebrews 4:14

YOU ARE THE GREAT SHEPHERD: Hebrews 13:20

YOU ARE THE GUIDE: Psalm 48:14

Early Morning Prayers

SCRIPTURE TO READ

"Have you commanded the morning since your days began, And caused the dawn to know its place..."
Job 38:12 , NKJV

PRAYERS

1. *Thank You, Lord, for a brand-new day.*
2. *Thank You, Father, for this beautiful day that You have made.*
3. *Thank You, Father, for the miracle of sleeping and waking up.*
4. *I decree and declare that this is the day that the Lord has made, and I will rejoice and be glad in it, in Jesus' name.*
5. According to Psalm 118: 24: "This is the day the LORD has made; We will rejoice and be glad in it." *I declare that I shall be glad and rejoice in this day.*
6. *I decree that I shall have joy throughout this day, in Jesus' name.*
7. *I decree and declare that joy shall be my portion in the name of Jesus.*
8. *I decree and declare that I shall go out with joy according to the word of God in* Isaiah 55:12:

"For you shall go out with joy, And be led out with peace; The mountains and the hills Shall break forth into singing before you, And all the trees of the field shall clap their hands."
Isaiah 55:12, NKJV

9. *I decree and declare that everything that God has created will cooperate with me today in the name of Jesus.*

10. *I decree and declare that the sun shall not harm in the day* Psalm 121:6

11. *I decree and declare that the moon shall not harm me in the night* Psalm 121:6

12. *I decree and declare that the Lord will keep me from all harm today* Psalm 121:7.

13. *I declare that as I go out today, The presence of the Lord will go with me, according to* Exodus 33:14-16

    "And He said, 'My Presence will go *with you,* and I will give you rest.'

    Then he said to Him, 'If Your Presence does not go *with us,* do not bring us up from here. For how then will it be known that Your people and I have found grace in Your sight, except You go with us? So we shall be separate, Your people and I, from all the people who *are* upon the face of the earth.'"
    Exodus 33:14-16, NKJV

14. *Father, I declare that I shall enjoy the daily loads of benefit that you have prepared for me today.*

    "Blessed *be* the Lord, *Who* daily loads us *with benefits,*
    The God of our salvation! *Selah."*
    Psalm 68:19, NKJV

15. *I declare that lines shall fall for me in pleasant places according to your word in Psalm 16:6.*

    "The lines have fallen to me in pleasant *places;* Yes, I have a good inheritance."
    Psalm 16:6, NKJV

Father, I declare that this day shall be a glorious day.

In Jesus' name, I pray. Amen.

Lord, I Present Myself to You

SCRIPTURE TO READ

"I beseech you therefore, brethren, by the mercies of God, that you present your bodies a living sacrifice, holy, acceptable to God, *which is* your reasonable service. And do not be conformed to this world, but be transformed by the renewing of your mind, that you may prove what *is* that good and acceptable and perfect will of God."

Romans 12:1-2, NKJV

PRAYERS TO PRAY

1. *Father, I present myself to You as a living sacrifice. Father, help me to live a holy life that is pleasing and acceptable to you, oh Lord. I desire to be a living sacrifice for You.*
2. *Father, I place my everyday life before You: my sleeping, my eating, my going to work, my walking around in life. I place them in your hands as an offering to You, Lord.*
3. *Help me to dedicate myself and all that I have to You and to Your service, oh God.*

4. *Help me to be holy and let my life be well pleasing to you in the name of Jesus.*

5. *Help me not to adjust to the culture and practices of the world. Help me to think before I do anything.*

6. *Help me to fix my attention on You so that I can be changed from the inside out, in Jesus' name I have prayed.*

7. *Father, help me to focus on godly values and ethical attitudes so I may know your will for me and prove Your good, acceptable, and perfect will for me.*

In Jesus' name I pray. Amen

Draw Me Near to You, Oh God

SCRIPTURE TO READ

"Draw near to God and He will draw near to you.Cleanse *your* hands, *you* sinners; and purify *your* hearts, *you* double-minded."
    James 4:8, NKJV

PRAYERS TO PRAY

1. *Lord, please draw me near to You as I constantly make an effort to draw near to You.*
2. *Lord, please help me to live a life free of sin. The Blood of Jesus washes away sins, so let the blood of Jesus wash away my sins and make my hands clean, oh Lord.*
3. *Lord, help me to lead a pure life, a life that pleases you, oh God.*
4. *Lord, help me to replace every desire to sin with a desire to experience your purity.*
5. *Lord, help me to resist the devil's attraction and distractions to sin, oh Lord. Help me not be distracted from serving You by what I hear.*

6. *Lord, help me not be distracted from serving You by what I see. When people condemn men and women of God in the news, let it not distract me from serving You, oh God.*
7. *Lord, help me to humble myself before you oh Lord so You can lift me up in honour.*
8. *Lord, Help me to recognize that all I am is because of You Lord. Help me to lean on your power and guidance as I live my daily life.*

In Jesus' name I pray. Amen.

Jesus, Be the Centre of My Life

SCRIPTURE TO READ

"For this reason I bow my knees to the Father of our Lord Jesus Christ, from whom the whole family in heaven and earth is named, that He would grant you, according to the riches of His glory, to be strengthened with might through His Spirit in the inner man, that Christ may dwell in your hearts through faith; that you, being rooted and grounded in love, may be able to comprehend with all the saints what *is* the width and length and depth and height— to know the love of Christ which passes knowledge; that you may be filled with all the fullness of God."
Ephesians 3:14-19, NKJV

PRAYERS TO PRAY

1. *Lord Jesus, please come and take your place in my heart. Make your home in my heart because You are all I need, Jesus.*
2. *Lord, let your presence fill my life. Let your presence surround me, oh God.*
3. *Lord, let my roots grow down into your love and keep me strongly connected to You.*

4. *Lord, give me the power to understand the full dimension of your love for me.*

In Jesus' name I pray. Amen.

Lord Make Me a Blessing

SCRIPTURE TO READ

"Now the Lord had said to Abram: 'Get out of your country, From your family And from your father's house, To a land that I will show you. I will make you a great nation; I will bless you And make your name great; And you shall be a blessing. I will bless those who bless you ,And I will curse him who curses you; And in you all the families of the earth shall be blessed.'"
 Genesis 12:1-3, NKJV

PRAYERS TO PRAY

1. *Father, please speak to me and give me direction every day of my life so that I can serve You faithfully.*
2. *Father, show me how to walk with you daily as Abram walked with You daily.*
3. *Father, speak to me personally as You spoke to Abram personally.*
4. *Father, please make me a great nation; let my life attract and retain greatness. Make me great in every area of my life.*
5. *Father, make me great in my academics, make me great in my career, make me great in my marriage, make me great in my*

ministry and in every area of my life, oh Lord, please make me great.

6. *Father, break all protocols for my sake and make me great, in Jesus' name.*

7. *Father, please make me a blessing, wherever I go, Lord, please make me a blessing. Make me a blessing to nations, make me a blessing to every town or city where I am located, in the name of Jesus I pray. Amen.*

8. *Father, make me a blessing to everyone I come in contact with. Make me a blessing to my family, make me a blessing to the church, make me a blessing to my colleagues, make me a blessing to strangers, make me a blessing to my generation, in Jesus' mighty name I pray.*

Amen

Lord, Help Me to Flourish Like a Palm Tree

SCRIPTURE TO READ

"The righteous shall flourish like a palm tree, He shall grow like a cedar in Lebanon. Those who are planted in the house of the LORD Shall flourish in the courts of our God. They shall still bear fruit in old age; They shall be fresh and flourishing."
Psalm 92:12-14, NKJV

PRAYERS TO PRAY

1. *Lord, please help me to flourish like the palm tree, to be strong and to live long, just like the palm tree.*
2. *Lord, make me an excellent source of spiritual nourishment to my generation, teach me Your Word and help me to teach others your Word.*
3. *Lord, help me to be productive, strong, and immovable no matter the circumstances around me.*
4. *Lord, as I place my faith firmly on You, let me have strength and vitality to serve you.*

5. *Lord, help me to continue to bear fruit throughout my lifetime. Even in old age, help me to bear fruits that will abide.*

In Jesus' name I pray. Amen.

Give Me a Clean Heart, Oh God

SCRIPTURE TO READ

"Create in me a clean heart, O God, And renew a steadfast spirit within me. Do not cast me away from Your presence, And do not take Your Holy Spirit from me. Restore to me the joy of Your salvation,

And uphold me *by Your* generous Spirit."
Psalm 51:10-12, NKJV

PRAYERS TO PRAY

1. *Lord, please create in me a clean heart. Oh God, purify my heart, make my heart become receptive to do your will.*
2. *Father, please take away the stony and stubborn heart from me. Give a heart that is obedient to You. Give me a heart that thinks pure thoughts.*
3. *Father, please wash away every negative and unproductive thoughts from my heart. Wash away thoughts of fear, thoughts of failure. Wash away thoughts of rejection, thoughts of sudden death, fear of the unknown. Lord, please wash away bad thoughts from my heart.*

4. *Father, fill my heart with thoughts of your goodness, thoughts of success.*
5. *Father, please give me a kind heart.*
6. *Father, please do not disconnect me from your presence.*
7. *Father, please make me willing to obey you and follow you.*

Prayer to Be Close to God

SCRIPTURE TO READ

"The LORD *is* near to those who have a broken heart, And saves such as have a contrite spirit."
    Psalm 34:18, NKJV

PRAYERS TO PRAY

1. *Lord, I surrender myself to **Y**our will, oh Lord. **F**orgive me of my sins, oh Lord.*
2. *Lord, I lay down all my burdens before you, Oh God. I pray that you will remove anything that has kept me far away from you in the past. Please remove that hindrance and accept me as your very own, in Jesus' name we pray.*
3. *Take away all my sins and wash me clean with the blood of Jesus.*
4. *I surrender my all to you. I repent of my sinful ways. Father, please draw me nearer to you.*

In Jesus' name I pray. Amen.

The Lord Will Preserve Me

"The LORD shall preserve your going out and your coming in
From this time forth, and even forevermore."
Psalm 121:8 NKJV

PRAYERS TO PRAY

1. *Thank You, Lord, for your preserving grace.*
2. *Thank You, Lord, for brand-new day.*
3. *I decree and declare safety over me and my family in our going
   out and coming in today in the name of Jesus. Psalm 121:8*
4. *I plead the blood of Jesus over my life, over my husband/wife and
   over my children in the name of Jesus.*
5. *I decree and declare that lines shall fall for me in pleasant places
   today in the name of Jesus. Psalm 16:6*
6. *I decree and declare that I shall enjoy the daily load of benefit that
   God has prepared for me today.*
7. *Thank You, Father, for the daily loads of benefit.*
8. *I decree and declare that the presence of the Lord will go with me
   and my family wherever I go today in Jesus name. Exodus 33:15*

9. *Father, let Your presence lead me to places of favour.*
10. *Father, please help me to be a blessing to someone today, in Jesus' name.*
11. *Father, please let my ways please you today and cause my enemies to be at peace with me.*

In Jesus' name I pray. Amen.

The Lord Is My Sustainer

SCRIPTURE TO READ

"I lay down and slept; I awoke, for the LORD sustained me."
  Psalms 3:5, NKJV

PRAYERS TO PRAY

1. *Thank You, Lord, for being my sustainer.*
2. *Thank You, Lord, for being my keeper and for watching over me in my sleep.*
3. *Thank You, Lord, for waking me up this morning. Some people slept and did not wake up to see another day.*
4. *Thank You, Lord, for the miracle of sleeping and waking up.*
5. *Thank You, Lord, for your mercies that are new every morning, according to your word in* Lamentations 3:22-23:
6. "Through the LORD's mercies we are not consumed, Because His compassions fail not. They are new every morning; Great is Your faithfulness."
7. Lamentations 3:22-23, NKJV

8. *Thank you, Lord, for the new song I have received in this scripture; Your mercies are new every morning, great is thy faithfulness.*

9. *Father, please continue to be my sustainer in life.*

In Jesus' name I pray. Amen.

Prayer to Delight
Yourself in the Lord

SCRIPTURE TO READ

"Delight yourself also in the LORD, And He shall give you the desires of your heart." Psalms 37:4, NKJV

PRAYERS TO PRAY

1. *Father Lord, help me to delight myself in you, Oh Lord.*
2. *Father Lord, help me to experience the joy and pleasure of being in Your presence in a greater dimension. I will not be weary, I will not be be slothful, in Jesus' name.*
3. *Father Lord, help me to seek You diligently. I pray that You will be diligent in seeking the Lord.*
4. *Father Lord, help me to overcome addiction— addiction to TV programs, addiction to sleep, addiction to the computer, addiction to Facebook.*
5. *Father Lord, help me to devote more time to serve You, Lord. Lord, help me to devote more quality time to my fellowship with You so I can know You better, in Jesus' name.*

6. *I pray that I will not be distracted in my service to You, oh Lord.*

7. *Lord, let me always be filled with the joy and peace that comes from being in Your presence.*

8. *Let my spiritual life improve and let it not collapse, in Jesus' name.*

9. *The fire of God upon my alter (my heart) will continue to burn. It will never go out, in Jesus' name.*

10. *I decree paralysis over all powers responsible for wandering thoughts during prayers and service. Be paralyzed in Jesus' name.*

11. *I decree paralysis over all powers responsible for heaviness of the spirit.*

12. *I decree paralysis over all powers responsible for distractions and inability to sincerely praise the Lord, in Jesus' mighty name.*

13. *I decree that my labour as a Christian will not be in vain. I will be steadfast, immovable, and always abound in the work of the Lord.*

In Jesus' name I pray. Amen.

Prayers for Divine Lifting

SCRIPTURE TO READ

"LORD, how they have increased who trouble me! Many are they who rise up against me. Many are they who say of me, 'There is no help for him in God.' Selah But You, O LORD, are a shield for me, My glory and the One who lifts up my head."
　　Psalms 3:1-3, NKJV

PRAYERS TO PRAY

1. *Father, be a shield for me, be the glory and the lifter of my head.*
2. *Lord, please lift my head from trouble when trouble comes my way. Oh God, make a way of escape for me.*
3. *Oh Lord God, lift my head from destruction.*
4. *Lord, please lift my head from shame and disgrace.*
5. *Lord, please lift my head from all the plans of the enemies.*
6. *Oh God, lift my head from all forms of evil.*

In Jesus' name I pray. Amen.

Prayers for Open Heavens

SCRIPTURE TO READ

"The next day, as they went on their journey and drew near the city, Peter went up on the housetop to pray, about the sixth hour. Then he became very hungry and wanted to eat; but while they made ready, he fell into a trance and saw heaven opened and an object like a great sheet bound at the four corners, descending to him and let down to the earth."
Acts 10:9-11, NKJV

PRAYERS TO PRAY

1. *Father, please open heavens upon me.*
2. *Lord, help me to operate under open heavens in every area of my life. Help me to operate under open heavens in my career, ministry, and family life.*
3. *Help me, Lord, to have a clear vision of You; a vision that is not blurring, a vision that is clear.*
4. *Open heavens upon my home, let my marriage experience open heaven, let all my family members enjoy the blessing of open heavens.*

5. *Open heavens upon my ministry and give me direction in my ministry so that I can serve you better.*
6. *Open heavens upon my children. Teach them your ways and help them to obey and serve you.*

In Jesus' name I pray. Amen

Prayer for Light

SCRIPTURE TO READ

"12 Then Jesus spoke to them again, saying, "I am the light of the world. He who follows Me shall not walk in darkness, but have the light of life."
John 8:12, NKJV

PRAYERS TO PRAY

1. *Light of the world, step into the dark areas of my life.*
2. *Light of the world, step into the secret sins of my life.*
3. *Light of the world, step into my secret faults.*
4. *Light of the world, step into my life and take away the faults in my life.*
5. *Let the God that destroys darkness destroy the activities of darkness in my life.*
6. *Just as darkness cannot stand light, Father, let every activity of darkness around me and my household be destroyed in Jesus' name.*
7. *Let your light shine and let every hatred be destroyed.*

8. *Let your light shine and let every evil be destroyed.*

In Jesus' name I pray. Amen.

Prayer to Be Transformed by the Light of God

SCRIPTURE TO READ

"As he journeyed he came near Damascus, and suddenly a light shone around him from heaven. Then he fell to the ground, and heard a voice saying to him, 'Saul, Saul, why are you persecuting Me?' And he said, 'Who are You, Lord?' Then the Lord said, 'I am Jesus, whom you are persecuting. It is hard for you to kick against the goads.' So he, trembling and astonished, said, 'Lord, what do You want me to do?' Then the Lord said to him, 'Arise and go into the city, and you will be told what you must do.'"
    Acts 9:3-6, NKJV

PRAYERS TO PRAY

1. *Oh Lord, transform me with the power of Your light.*
2. *Oh Lord, transform my heart with the power of Your light.*
3. *Oh Lord, transform my thoughts' process by the power of Your Light*
4. *Oh Lord, transform my desires by the power of Your light*

5. *Oh Lord, let Your light transform me from the inside out*
6. *Father, make me over again in Your light.*

In Jesus' name I pray. Amen.

Lord Make Me a Light
to the Gentiles

SCRIPTURE TO READ

"I, the LORD, have called You in righteousness, And will hold Your hand; I will keep You and give You as a covenant to the people, As a light to the Gentiles."
Isaiah 42:6, NKJV.

PRAYERS TO PRAY

1. *Father, empower me to keep your light shining.*
2. *Oh Light of God, arise and illuminate my environment and disperse the darkness surrounding me.*
3. *Destroy every work of darkness around me.*
4. *Father, transform me with your light, oh God.*
5. *Father, let your light shine in my heart to keep me from error and sin.*
6. *Make me a light to the gentiles.*
7. *Father, transform me with your light as You transformed Paul of tarsus by Your light.*

8. *Destroy the evil intentions of my heart with Your light.*
9. *Father, let your light shine in every area of my life.*
10. *In any area where darkness is still prevailing, Lord, let your light shine.*
11. *Let Your light shine in me that people may see your good works in me and glorify You.*

In Jesus' name I pray. Amen.

Prayer to Remain Relevant to God

SCRIPTURE TO READ

"And Samuel went no more to see Saul until the day of his death. Nevertheless Samuel mourned for Saul, and the LORD regretted that He had made Saul king over Israel."
　1 Samuel 15:35, NKJV

PRAYERS TO PRAY

1. *Lord, please help to remain relevant in your service.*
2. *Lord, help me to continue to obey you and serve You faithfully.*
3. *Lord, help me to follow Your leading and directions always.*
4. *Lord, please help me to always find favor in Your sight.*
5. *Lord, help me to do only the things that please you.*
6. *Lord, please help me to subdue pride and worldly knowledge and to trust you to direct my paths in life.*

In Jesus' name I pray. Amen.

Prayer to Serve God

SCRIPTURE TO READ

"I planted, Apollos watered, but God gave the increase."
I Corinthians 3:6 , NKJV
"Now he who plants and he who waters are one, and each one will receive his own reward according to his own labor. For we are God's fellow workers; you are God's field, you are God's building."
I Corinthians 3:8-9, NKJV

PRAYERS TO PRAY

1. *Father, let me not lose my reward, in Jesus' name.*
2. *Help me to serve You faithfully to the end.*
3. *Father, please help me to be a true representative of Christ.*
4. *Lord, let the world see Jesus in me wherever I go.*
5. *Lord, showcase Your glory, beauty, and power through me.*
6. *Lord, help me not lead people astray*
7. *Lord, let the world see Jesus in my life and let my light shine.*

In Jesus' name I pray. Amen

Lord, Order My Steps

SCRIPTURE TO READ

"The steps of a good man are ordered by the LORD, And He delights in his way."
Psalms 37:23, NKJV

PRAYERS TO PRAY

1. *Father, order my steps this season. Direct me, Lord, to be at the right place at the right time.*
2. *Lord, help me to be at the right place at the right time.*
3. *Lord, please do not let me be in a place where Your grace does not take me.*
4. *Father, fill me anew with your Spirit.*
5. *Spirit of the Living God, fall upon me.*
6. *Make me over again and renew my heart.*
7. *Father, help me to be diligent in serving you, oh Lord, according to your word in* 2 Timothy 2:15:
   "Be diligent to present yourself approved to God, a worker who does not need to be ashamed, rightly dividing the word of truth."

8. *Father, help me to present myself to You as a worker that is not ashamed of the gospel of Jesus.*

   "For I am not ashamed of the gospel of Christ, for it is the power of God to salvation for everyone who believes, for the Jew first and also for the Greek."

   Romans 1:16, NKJV

9. *Father, give me a garment of praise against the spirit of heaviness, oh God.*

10. *Father, give me double for every trouble.*

    "Instead of your shame you shall have double honor, And instead of confusion they shall rejoice in their portion. Therefore in their land they shall possess double; Everlasting joy shall be theirs."

    Isaiah 61:7, NKJV

11. *Father, disappoint all my disappointment.*

12. *Father, frustrate all my frustrations in Jesus' name.* "He frustrates the devices of the crafty, So that their hands cannot carry out their plans.

    Job 5:12, NKJV

13. *Lord, please answer my prayers and give me results that will silence all my mockers.*

14. *Lord, please answer my prayers and give me results that will put an end to every insult in my life.*

In Jesus' name I pray. Amen.

Use Me for Your Glory Lord

SCRIPTURE TO READ

"⁸ Also I heard the voice of the Lord, saying:
   'Whom shall I send,
   And who will go for Us?'
   Then I said, 'Here *am* I! Send me.'"
   Isaiah 6:8, NKJV

PRAYERS TO PRAY

Declare to the Lord and say, "Lord, I'm available to you."

Song by Patience Iwoh
Lord, I'm available to you
Lord, I'm available to you
Use me for your glory
I'm available to you
Use me for your glory
I'm available to you.

1.   *Father Lord, I am available for you. Use me for your glory, Lord.*

2. *Father, use me in any way you want to use me.*
3. *Father, I surrender my all to you.*
4. *Father, please use me as your oracle to declare your word; use me to prophesy to the nations.*
5. *Father, please use me to declare the good news of Jesus.*
6. *Father, please use me to declare your greatness in all the nations of the world.*

In Jesus' name I pray. Amen.

Open the Heavens Oh Lord

SCRIPTURE TO READ

"Oh, that You would rend the heavens! That You would come down! That the mountains might shake at Your presence—"
  Isaiah 64:1, NKJV

PRAYERS TO PRAY

1. *Father, open the heavens upon me. Heavens upon my life be opened.*
2. *Oh Lord, please let mountains shake at your presence, Lord.*
3. *Lord, let every mountain of weakness shake at Your presence. Let them crumble, in Jesus' name*
4. *Lord, let every mountain of sickness shake at Your presence. Let them crumble, in Jesus' name*
5. *Lord, let every mountain of hard, fruitless labour shake at Your presence. Let them crumble, in Jesus' name*
6. *Lord, let every mountain of disobedience shake at Your presence. Let them crumble, in Jesus' name.*

7. *Let the mountains shake at your presence and crumble.*

In Jesus' name I pray. Amen.

Prayer for the Church

SCRIPTURE TO READ

"And it shall come to pass afterward That I will pour out My Spirit on all flesh; Your sons and your daughters shall prophesy, Your old men shall dream dreams, Your young men shall see visions."
   Joel 2:28, NKJV

PRAYERS TO PRAY

1. *Father, let your power flow in the church.*
2. *Let your power flow in our lives today.*
3. *Like in the day of Pentecost, let your power flow, oh Lord.*
4. *Like in the days of old, let your power flow, oh Lord.*
5. *Release the power to do the impossible in our midst.*
6. *Holy Spirit, move in our lives today.*
7. *Release the power to heal the sick. Let your healing power flow.*
8. *Father, let there be miracles, signs, and wonders occurring in the church.*
9. *Father, heal the sick, raise the dead, deliver the oppressed.*

In Jesus' name I pray. Amen.

Lord Make Me a Pacesetter

SCRIPTURE TO READ

"⁷ in all things showing yourself *to be* a pattern of good works; in doctrine *showing* integrity, reverence, incorruptibility, [a]"
   Titus 2:7, NKJV

PRAYERS TO PRAY

1. *Father, please make me a spiritual pacesetter so that millions may come to Your Kingdom through me.*
2. *As a worker in the church, Lord, please take me to a greater height. Oh Lord, make me a pacesetter.*
3. *As a leader in the church, Lord, please take me to a greater height. Oh Lord, make me a pacesetter.*
4. *As a pastor, Lord, please take me to a greater height, oh Lord. Make me a pacesetter.*
5. *Lord, please take me to a greater height, oh Lord. Please make me a pacesetter to the congregation.*
6. *Lord, make me an answer to someone's prayers this year.*
7. *Let me become an agent of divine surprises to others.*
8. *Let my problems become the solution that people are looking for.*

9. *Father, let every department and ministry in my church flourish and serve You faithfully.*
10. *Lord, I pray that the leaders and minister in the church will not fail You.*
11. *I pray that the pastors will not fail God.*
12. *I Pray that members of congregation will come to church prepared to hear from God and not to hear from man.*

In Jesus' name I pray. Amen.

Purify Me with Your Fire, Oh God

SCRIPTURE TO READ

"Everything that can endure fire, you shall put through the fire, and it shall be clean; and it shall be purified with the water of purification. But all that cannot endure fire you shall put through water."
Numbers 31:23, NKJV

PRAYERS TO PRAY

1. *Holy Spirit, take over my life, my heart, my soul.*
2. *Holy Ghost fire, do the work of purification in my life.*
3. *Let everything that needs to shaken by the Holy Spirit be shaken and emptied out of my life in the name of Jesus.*

"For thus says the Lord of hosts: 'Once more (it is a little while) I will shake heaven and earth, the sea and dry land; and I will shake all nations, and they shall come to the Desire of All Nations, and I will fill this temple with glory,' says the Lord of hosts.
Haggai 2:6, 7, NKJV

"Now this, 'Yet once more,' indicates the removal of those things that are being shaken, as of things that are made, that the things which cannot be shaken may remain."
Hebrews 12:27, NKJV

4. *Let everything that needs to be shaken and removed be removed from my life by the power of the Holy Spirit in the name of Jesus.*

5. *Holy Ghost, incubate me in Your fire.*

6. *Lord, search me and know my heart and my intentions.*

"Search me, O God, and know my heart; Try me, and know my anxieties; And see if there is any wicked way in me, And lead me in the way everlasting."
Psalms 139:23, 24, NKJV

7. *Lord, please answer me by fire today. Lord, please let Your fire burn away every affliction in my life.*

8. *Lord, please let Your fire burn away every limitation in my life.*

In Jesus' name I pray. Amen.

Prayer of Thanksgiving

PRAYERS TO PRAY

1. *Thank God for daily blessings.*

   "Blessed be the Lord, Who daily loads us with benefits, The God of our salvation! Selah." Psalm 68:19, NKJV

   "Bless the Lord, O my soul: and all that is within me, bless his holy name. Bless the Lord, O my soul, and forget not all his benefits: Who forgiveth all thine iniquities; who healeth all thy diseases; Who redeemeth thy life from destruction; who crowneth thee with lovingkindness and tender mercies; Who satisfieth thy mouth with good things; so that thy youth is renewed like the eagle's."

   Psalm 103:1-5, KJV

2. *Thank God for safety and protection over us and our families.*

   "No evil shall befall you, Nor shall any plague come near your dwelling…"

   Psalm 91:10, NKJV

3. *Let's thank the Lord for deliverance from the plans of the enemy.*

   "So shall they fear The name of the Lord from the west, And His glory from the rising of the sun; When the enemy comes in like a flood, The Spirit of the Lord will lift up a standard against him.

Isaiah 59:19, NKJV

4. *Thank God for setting you apart and not allowing your enemies to harm you. Thank God for the mark of God upon you.*

"When they went from one nation to another, From one kingdom to another people, He permitted no one to do them wrong; Yes, He rebuked kings for their sakes, Saying, Do not touch My anointed ones, And do My prophets no harm."

Psalm 105:13-15, NKJV

Almighty God, we thank you, we give you praise for all you have done. Thank you for safety and protection. Thank you for daily blessings. Thank you for deliverances.

In Jesus' name I pray. Amen.

Prayer for Children

"All your children shall be taught by the Lord and great shall be the peace of your children."
   Isaiah 54:13

PRAYERS TO PRAY

1. *Father Lord, please teach my children your ways and let their peace be great.*
2. *Lord, please give them an ear that is attentive to your word.*
3. *Lord, please give them a heart that hungers and thirsts after your righteousness.*
4. *Help my children to love you.*
5. *Make all my children to be for signs and for wonders, oh Lord according to your word in* Isaiah 8:18
6. *Lord, please make my children to grow like Jesus grew in stature and found favour with men and with God.* Luke 2:52
7. *Establish my children in righteousness, oh Lord, and let the destiny of my children be fulfilled.*

8. *Lord, please draw my children to Yourself and help them to stay connected to you always.*

9. *May my children delight in your presence, may they find joy and peace in your presence, and may they never run away from your presence.*

10. *Father, please heal the backsliding of my children.*

11. *Father, let your presence always be with my children wherever they go, in Jesus' name. Amen.* Exo 33:15

12. *Lord, please keep my children from evil and keep evil away from them, in Jesus' name. Amen.*

13. *Lord, please make my sons flourish in their youth like well-nurtured plants.* Psalm 144:12

14. *Lord, please make my daughters like graceful pillars carved to beautify a palace. Make them to be pillars in the house of God.* Psalm 144:12.

15. *Lord, please establish my children in righteousness, keep my children far from oppression and from any form of terror.* Isaiah 54:14

In Jesus' name I pray. Amen.

Oh Lord, Give Me a New Song

SCRIPTURE TO READ

"When the LORD brought back the captivity of Zion,

We were like those who dream. Then our mouth was filled with laughter, and our tongue with singing. Then they said among the nations,

'The LORD has done great things for them.' The LORD has done great things for us, *and* we are glad."

Psalm 126: 1-3

PRAYERS TO PRAY

1. *Father, I declare that as from today, I will sing a new song for the rest of my life.*
   I will sing a new song of victory
   I will sing a new song of joy
   I will sing a new song of favor
   I will sing a new song of promotion
   I will sing a new song of healing
   I will sing a new song of miracles
   I will sing a new song of signs and wonders in Jesus' name

2. *Father, deliver me from captivity of sin and give me a new song to sing, in Jesus' name.*

3. *Father, deliver me from captivity of sickness and give me a new song to sing, in Jesus' name.*

4. *Father, deliver me from captivity of fear and give me a new song to sing, in Jesus' name.*

5. *Father, deliver me from every form of captivity and give me a new song to sing, in Jesus' name.*

In Jesus' name I pray. Amen.

Prayers for Peace

SCRIPTURE TO READ

"The Lord will lift up His countenance upon you and give you peace in Jesus name.

The LORD lift up His countenance upon you, and give you peace.'" Numbers 6:26

Now may the Lord of peace Himself give you peace always in every way. The Lord *be* with you all."

2 Thess 3:16

PRAYERS TO PRAY

1. *Oh Lord, give me peace in every area of my life.*
2. *Oh Lord, give me peace in my home according to your word in Job 5:24.*
3. *Oh Lord, give me peace in my career, let me experience peace with my colleagues. Let me experience peace in my marriage.*
4. *Oh Lord, let my children experience great peace. Isaiah 54:13*
5. *Oh Lord, give me peace in my ministry.*
6. *Oh Lord, give me great peace. Psalm 119:165*
7. *Oh Lord, please deliver me in every battle of life. Psalm 55:18*

8. *Oh Lord, please make my enemies to be at peace with me. Pro 16:7*

9. *Oh Lord, please make my home a peaceful habitation. Isa 32:18*

10. *My home shall be peaceful in Jesus' name. Psalm 122:7*

11. *Oh Lord, please give me peace while I am asleep and awake. Psalm 4:8, Psalm 3:5*

12. *Oh Lord, please cause everything that you have created to cooperate with me and be at peace with me in Jesus' name. Job 5:23-24.*

13. *Oh Lord, make me and my family to enjoy your peace every day of our lives.*

In Jesus' name I pray. Amen.

Prayer for Favour

SCRIPTURE TO READ

"Remember me, O Lord, with the favor You have toward Your people.
Oh, visit me with Your salvation."
Psalm 106:4, NKJV

PRAYERS TO PRAY

1. *Oh Lord, remember with favor and bless me.*
2. *Oh Lord, favor me in my career and business.*
3. *Oh Lord, favor me in my marriage and in the life of my children.*
4. *Oh Lord, favor me and answer my prayer; make the work of my hands prosper.*
5. *Oh Lord, remember me and answer my prayers.*
6. *Oh Lord, remember me and remove every long-standing problem from my life.*
7. *Oh Lord, remember me as you remembered Sarah, and bless me with children.*
8. *Oh Lord, remember me as you remembered Hannah, and bless me with children.*

9. *Oh Lord, remember me as you remembered Rachel, and bless me with children.*

10. *Oh Lord, remember me and favor me in every area of my life.*

11. *Oh Lord, please silence all my mockers, in Jesus' name.*

In Jesus' name I pray. Amen.